The Kayak Express!
with 250+ visual aids

Aquatics Unlimited, Inc.
Boston, MA

Written by Mark B. Solomon.

Edited by Gary B. Solomon.

Black & white photography by Robert Tannenbaum.

Color photography by Robert Tannenbaum.

Photography assistance by L. Harvey and A. Lynn.

Graphic artwork by Mark B. Solomon.

Flat water shot on location at Camp Avoda, Middleboro, MA.
White water shot on the Androscoggin River, Errol, NH.

Kayak equipment graciously provided by Perception™ Kayaks.

Special thanks to Paul Davis, Tom Leavitt, Andrea Parker, Gregory Smith, and the Camp Avoda small craft department.

Published by Aquatics Unlimited, Inc., Boston, MA.

Distributed by: ICS Books, Inc, 1370 E. 86th Place, Merrillville, IN 46410 (800) 541-7323

Printed in USA

Preface

The four sections of *The Kayak Express!* are individual learning units. The student learns a complete skill set in each section: kayaking knowledge tools, kayaking practical skills, and kayaking strokes. Each section builds upon the skills taught in the previous section. The review questions and answers allow the student to measure his or her learning progress.

Beginner Section:
The Beginner Section is designed to educate the student in flat water kayaking fundamentals. At the end of the Beginner Section, the student should be able, under supervision, to safely enter and exit the kayak, paddle in a straight line, and safely return back to shore!

Intermediate Section:
The Intermediate Section is designed to educate the student in practical kayaking issues. At the end of the Intermediate Section, the student should be able to perform all basic flat water strokes!

Advanced Section:
The Advanced Section is designed to educate the student in additional kayaking topics. At the end of the Advanced Section, the student, under supervision, should be able to roll a kayak!

River Paddler Section:
The River Paddler Section is designed to educate the student in river basics. At the end of the River Paddler Section, the student, with an experienced white water river guide, should be able to select, scout, read, and paddle a Class 2 white water river!

Paddlers are encouraged to practice the practical and paddling skills taught in the order the skills are presented. Practice of each skill should continue until the paddler has become proficient at the skill. For example, until the paddler can perform a wet exit while relaxed, the paddler should continue wet exit practice before moving to the strokes section. And, until the paddler can paddle in a straight line, he or she should continue straight line paddling before continuing to the next skill. Paddlers must, for their own safety, repeatedly practice each skill and advance at a comfortable pace. Before starting river paddling, we recommend continuing flat water paddling until the paddler has fully developed each and every flat water paddling skill.

The Kayak Express! leads the student through basic white water paddling by teaching elementary skills and strokes on safe flat water. Though many of the safety, practical skills, and paddling skills transfer to touring and sea kayaking, this book focuses on slalom kayaking for flat and white water paddling.

We dedicate this book to our parents, Barbara and Leonard Solomon, for providing us the opportunity to spend our childhood years at summer camp, for being our education role models, and for being so supportive throughout *"The Kayak Express!"* project.

Table of Contents

Table of Contents

Aquatics Unlimited presents *The Kayak Express!* and your kayaking instructors, Mark and Gary.

Welcome aboard! Today we'll be learning the finer points of kayaking: everything from kayak nomenclature and high braces to reading the river and eddy turns!

Figure 1. Your kayaking instructors, Mark and Gary

That's right, Mark. This will be an exciting day on the water, as always. We'll be covering all that you mentioned and much more in our outdoor classroom. Don't worry if Mark's words sounded foreign; *by the end of this course, we'll all be speaking the same language.*

Figure 2. White water paddling

Beginner Introduction

- safety
- use of PFD
- clothing
- recommended safety equipment

Safety is just another word for common sense, and in kayaking, like all watersports, one must always be prepared for the unexpected.

Figure 3. Unexpected event

I'm helping Lara put on a Type II **PFD**, or personal flotation device. We listen for the click, adjust the fit, and tie the top in a bow.

Figure 4. Listen for the click and adjust the fit

Figure 5. Secure the PFD by tying the top in a bow

Always be sure that you are wearing a PFD correctly rated for your weight. This information can be found on the **Coast Guard approval label** located on the rear of the PFD.

The difference between Lara's Type II PFD and Gary's Type III PFD is head support. The **Type II PFD** is designed to keep the wearer's breathing passages clear of the water if the wearer is freely floating in the water while unconscious.

Figure 6. Unconscious boater with Type II PFD

A **Type IJI PFD** is often worn while kayaking because it offers more movement freedom than the Type II PFD. The decision to wear a Type III PFD or a Type II PFD should be based on the user's boating experience, swimming proficiency, and the weather and water conditions.

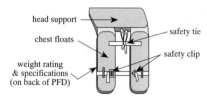

Figure 7. Type II PFD

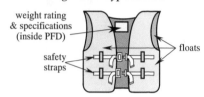

Figure 8. Type III FPD

Maintain the PFD's safety qualities by hanging it to dry, keeping it clean, and especially *not* using it as a seat cushion. *Be good to your PFD, it may just save your life.*

Wearing either **booties** or **shoes** with non-skid soles protects feet from injury and reduces the likelihood of slipping on wet surfaces. In kayaking, shoes also help to hold one's feet firmly to the foot pedals while paddling. For river paddling, paddlers must wear foot protection because of the unfamiliar shoreline debris and river obstructions that can injure feet if unprotected.

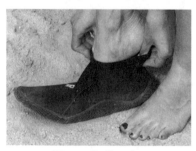

Figure 9. Booties

Figure 10. Non-skid soled shoes, sunglasses, sunscreen

A high numbered **sunscreen** correct for your skin type should be applied before kayaking.

Wearing **sunglasses** with **UV protection** is a must to protect the eyes from water glare.

Figure 11. Use sunscreen   *Figure 12. Wear sunglasses*

Wearing appropriate **clothing** will make our boating experience more comfortable, but good judgement in this regard also protects us from **medical conditions**, such as **sunstroke**, **heat exhaustion**, and **hypothermia**. For example, a wetsuit or drysuit is mandatory gear when the air and water temperatures do not add up to 100°F (38°C). However, cold water can quickly drain a paddler's strength, so paddlers should be overcautious when paddling on cold water. We recommend seeking current medical literature on the dangers which can result from prolonged exposure to the elements.

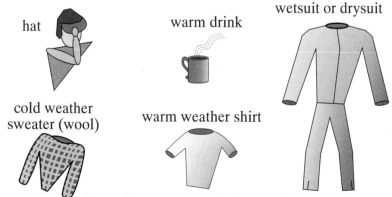

Figure 13. Appropriate clothing and drinks

The required and recommended **safety equipment** is as important as proper protection from the elements. Prepared paddlers always have audible and visible **distress signals** available on the craft and are informed of current **waterway regulations**. We recommend taking extra line, a heaving line, a spare PFD, a bailer (usually a **sponge** when kayaking), and, of course, a **first aid kit**. Consult with the local waterway authorities and outfitters in the area you will be kayaking to be sure you know all the current rules, regulations, and water conditions.

Figure 14. Audible and visible distress signals

Common sense suggests knowing your limits. Recognize your abilities, be aware of other craft, shallow water, rocks, and other obstructions. Always inform someone on shore that you are on the water, and have **proper supervision**. Be prepared to use your audible and visible distress signals in case of an emergency.

Figure 15. Flat water safety equipment

Beginner Tools

- **kayak nomenclature**
- **paddle nomenclature**
- **choosing a paddle**

Tools are important for getting a job done. **Kayak nomenclature**, or names of parts of the kayak, is a paddler's most important communication tool. Let's review some kayak nomenclature basics...

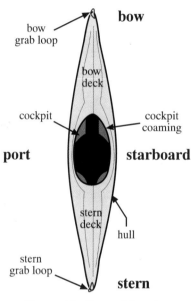

Figure 16. General kayak nomenclature

Let's begin with the general parts of the craft. The front of the kayak is known as the **bow**. The rear of the kayak is referred to as the **stern**. The side to paddler's left is called the **port** - note four letters in port and left - and the **starboard** is the side to paddler's right. The area inside the kayak is referred to as the **cockpit** and the rim around the cockpit is the **cockpit coaming**. The bottom of the kayak is known as the **hull**. The top of the kayak in front of the cockpit is known as the **bow deck**, and the top of the kayak behind the cockpit is referred to as the **stern deck**. The loops of line or straps found at the bow and stern are the bow and stern **grab loops**, respectively.

Paddlers should also be familiar with some specific parts within the kayak. The paddler sits on the kayak **seat**, and the paddler's feet press against **foot pedals**, also referred to as **foot braces**. The paddler can adjust the foot pedals toward the bow or stern by sliding each along its **foot pedal rail**. **Flotation bags**, typically two in the bow and two in the stern, are filled by blowing air into the **flotation bag fill tubes**, and the air is kept in a bag by closing its **fill tube valve**. The flotation bags are designed to keep a capsized kayak from completely filling with water and sinking. A **capsized kayak** refers to a kayak that is floating upside down or is floating right side up but semi-filled with water. To help retain hull shape, a kayak has **foam walls** in the bow and stern that extend from the **hull**, or bottom of the kayak, to the deck. **Knee pads** made of either soft rubber or neoprene are often placed beneath the bow deck, such that a paddler's knees will be cushioned while paddling.

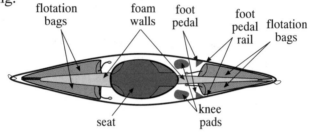

Figure 17. Internal kayak parts

Kayak **paddle nomenclature** is also useful when communicating with other paddlers. The **shaft** is the pole the paddler holds. The paddler's hands hold the shaft at the **grips** when paddling, and the **neck**, or **throat**, is located where the shaft meets the **blades**, which are the flat or slightly curved pieces at each end of the paddle. The thin sides of the blades are simply referred to as the **edges**. The broad, flat sides of the blades are known as the **faces**, and the extreme end of each blade is called the **tip**. The blades are offset between 60° and 90° to reduce wind resistance while paddling. Slicing a blade through the air is known as **feathering**.

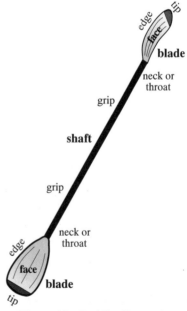

Figure 18. Paddle illustration

Now that we know paddle nomenclature, we can more easily discuss three methods for **choosing the correct paddle size** (for white water paddles only).

1. Place a blade tip on your shoe; the hand of an arm bent 90° at the elbow should be at the center of the shaft.

Figure 19. Choosing a paddle - tip on shoe

2. Hold a paddle throat and opposite blade tip; both arms should be straight.

Figure 20. Choosing a paddle - holding throat and tip

3. Hold the paddle on the grips over your head; both arms should make 90 degree bends.

Figure 21. Choosing a paddle - elbows angled 90°

height	whitewater	touring
5'-5'3"	196-200cm	210-220cm
5'4"-5'7"	198-202cm	215-225cm
5'8"-5'11"	200-204cm	220-230cm
6'-6'3"	202-206cm	225-240cm
6'4"-6'7"	204-208cm	240cm

Figure 22. Paddle size chart

Proper paddle size is important because the paddler needs to be comfortable while paddling. In general, a beginner paddler can use the paddle sizing methods or the chart above, but as a paddler becomes more advanced, he or she will want to use different length paddles for different paddling conditions. For example, river paddlers will use shorter paddles to enable quicker response to the uncertain turbulence of the river, or they may choose longer paddles for more power. In any event, only the paddler will know what length is comfortable for him or her. As a point of reference, the paddles Gary and Mark are using are 202 and 204 centimeters (approximately 80 inches) in length.

Beginner Practical

- portaging the kayak
- entering/exiting the kayak
- wet exit
- draining the kayak

Because kayaks are kept out of the water when not in use, the paddler should be familiar with some methods of **portaging** - a paddler's way of saying **carrying a kayak**. When performing any method of hand-carry portage, paddlers should lift and lower the kayaks using his or her legs while maintaining a straight back, so as not to strain back muscles. "Using the legs" means the paddler will bend his or her knees rather than bending at the waist.

The first method of portaging is the **suitcase carry**. The paddler turns the kayak on its side with the cockpit facing away from him or her, then uses one hand to hold the kayak at his or her carry-arm side. The suitcase carry is useful for medium length portages.

Figure 23. Portaging - suitcase carry

Figure 24. Portaging - thigh carry

In the **thigh carry**, the paddler holds the cockpit coaming on one side with both hands while the kayak hull bottom rests comfortably above the knees. Walking sideways rather than walking forward when using the thigh carry portaging method keeps the kayak from rotating. The thigh carry is useful for short portages.

18

Another type of carry is the **one-shoulder carry**, which makes walking with the kayak less cumbersome. The paddler places the kayak-side knee on the ground, hoists the cockpit to this shoulder, then stands. The other hand is available to carry the paddle or other gear.

Figure 25. Portaging - shoulder carry

A **two-person carry** makes a portage a much easier task than it is for a single paddler because the weight of the kayak is shared by the paddlers. In the two-person carry, each paddler holds the kayak by the end or the grabloop and walks comfortably. The **two-person two-kayak carry** is also very manageable for two people and ideal for long portages.

Figure 26. Portaging - two person, one kayak carry

Figure 27. Portaging - two person, two kayak carry

Paddlers who have never been in a kayak are often surprised by how easily kayaks roll on the water's surface, most noticeably during entry and upright exit. Therefore, when **entering the kayak**, paddlers should follow a procedure to keep the craft stable. Let's watch Mark demonstrate a safe kayak entry. First, Mark places the kayak alongside the shoreline. Second, he lays one shaft across the stern deck such that the other blade is resting on the shore. Third, Mark shifts his weight over the kayak and sits on the stern deck with his feet in the cockpit to each side of the bow foam wall. The paddler should attempt to clean off as much sand as possible from his or her booties before placing them into the cockpit, to reduce potential paddling

Figure 28. Entering the kayak- using the paddle for support

discomfort and tedious cleaning. Fourth, Mark places his hands behind him; one hand presses firmly down on the paddle shaft toward the blade resting on the shore, and the other holds the cockpit coaming and paddle shaft. Fifth, Mark straightens his knees, point his toes forward, and lowers himself from the stern deck into the cockpit.

Figure 29. Entering the kayak - straighten knees & point toes

Now that we know how to enter a kayak, the next skill to learn is the **kayak exit in the upright position**, also known as the **dry exit**. With the kayak next to the shore, simply reverse the process for entering the kayak. Place the shaft across the stern deck with one blade on the shore. Place hands on the paddle shaft and stern deck, straighten knees, point toes, push up to sit on the stern deck, then slowly shift body weight to the shore.

Figure 30. Exiting the kayak - reverse the entering procedure

The other and more important exit procedure with which a Beginner Paddler should become very familiar is the **wet exit**. In fact, the wet exit is such an important skill that no Beginner Paddler should be allowed to paddle without being fully briefed and fully rehearsed in the performance of the wet exit. The wet exit is used when the kayak has turned upside-down and the paddler wishes to remove him or herself from the kayak. The wet exit procedure is similar to the upright exit except now the paddler will be upside down. A spotter should be standing in the water beside the Beginner Paddler's kayak when learning and practicing the wet exit, in case of an emergency.

The **wet exit drill** is used to train a Beginner Paddler in the wet exit. The wet exit drill can be broken down into four distinct parts: set up, self-capsize, upside-down position, and wet exit. To ensure safety, this drill is required to be done a minimum of *three comfortable times*. Because of the number of times the paddler will be turning upside-down to perfect the wet exit, some paddlers choose to wear a pair of **swimming goggles** and **nose-clips** when learning the wet exit. Before moving on, however, paddlers who have chosen to wear swimming goggles and/or nose-clips must perform three comfortable wet exits without either device because those may not always be worn in an unexpected capsizing event.

Before beginning the wet exit drill, let's set some ground rules. In the Beginner Section, we will not be wearing a sprayskirt, so neither will we when learning the wet exit. Also, when practicing the wet exit, paddlers should put the paddle in a location that will not interfere with any portion of the drill; paddle placement locations could be the shore, dock, or floating in the water. If, while upside-down, there is any problem, the paddler should thump his or her hands on the surface-side of the kayak to inform the **spotter** (the assisting person standing in the water) that assistance is needed. Finally, be careful to choose a section of water deep enough so that the paddler does not hit head his or her head on the waterway bottom when upside down.

Let's watch Gary and Mark perform the wet exit drill. Gary, acting as Mark's spotter, will ensure Mark's safety. In the **wet exit drill** *set up*, Mark tucks forward and places both hands beneath the kayak. The tuck reduces the likelihood of his head hitting the waterway bottom and also puts Mark in the right position for performing the wet exit. Holding onto the kayak keeps Mark seated in the kayak, which will be the case when wearing the sprayskirt. The last part of the wet exit set up is for the paddler to tell the spotter he or she is ready to capsize.

Figure 31. Wet exit - tuck and roll

To begin the **wet exit drill** *self-capsize*, Mark simply shifts his body weight over the water. Mark takes a deep breath before submerging and maintains the tucked position with hands holding the kayak hull until the kayak is resting upside-down. Gary, as spotter, did a check on water depth and watches the paddler the entire way.

In the **wet exit drill** *upside-down position*, Mark remains calm, slowly exhales through his nose to prevent water from entering the nasal passages, **taps three times** on the hull, and gives Gary the **"thumbs up" signal**. The three taps and thumbs-up is requested to keep a paddler thinking about what he or she is doing in an effort to avoid panic and to indicate to the spotter a readiness to wet exit.

Figure 32. Wet exit - tapping the hull

Figure 33. Wet exit - thumbs up

Any more than three taps is an indication to the spotter that the paddler requires assistance. In the event of more than three taps, the spotter should immediately roll the kayak to the upright position, which should bring the paddler up with the kayak if he or she holds the bottom of the kayak, or safely dislodge the paddler from the cockpit if he or she does not hold the kayak.

In the **wet exit drill** *wet exit*, Mark places both hands on the stern deck, straightens his knees, points toes forward, pushes his body off the seat, and rolls to the side of the kayak in a somersault motion. Keeping his knees straight and toes pointed to the bow allows Mark's legs to pass through the cockpit unfettered. Rolling forward and to the side of the kayak allows Mark's PFD to assist him safely to the water's surface. In the event Mark had become disoriented, he would have relaxed, blown some air bubbles, and followed them to the water's surface.

Figure 34. Wet exit - forward somersault to the surface

All paddlers must practice, practice, practice the wet exit until comfortable and confident in exiting an overturned kayak.

After the wet exit, the kayak will often contain enough water to require the paddler to drain it, referred to as **draining the kayak**. If the paddler has a spotter available, the two can easily drain the kayak by raising up one end, then lowering it and raising the other end, in succession. The end should be raised slowly and smoothly to maintain balance as the water will tend to swirl and pour into the lower end, which will swiftly increase the weight on the lower end being supported by the other person. To avoid injury, paddlers should avoid raising the kayak end above their shoulders.

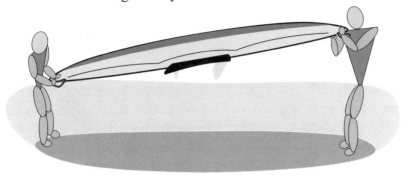

Figure 35. Draining the kayak with a partner

One way for a single paddler to drain the kayak is to raise one end of the kayak while balancing the other end on a dock, land, or the water's surface. A lot of water in the kayak will flow out through the cockpit, but to remove the remaining water in the kayak, the paddler must turn the kayak to be cockpit face up, lower the end being raised, allow the water to flow to the paddler's end, turn the kayak to be cockpit face down, and repeat the draining process. Two or three draining cycles may be necessary, depending on the paddler's tolerance to paddling with water in the kayak.

Figure 36. Draining the kayak without assistance

Beginner Strokes

- **using a paddle**
- **forward power stroke**
- **body position**
- **reverse stroke**

- **turning theory**
- **forward sweep**
- **reverse sweep**
- **paddling a straight course**

In the Beginner Strokes section, we will be learning how to use the paddle, paddle in a straight line, and spin a kayak (to return to shore). Since the paddling straight and spinning skills do not involve leaning the kayak on its side and we have not learned yet to wet exit with a sprayskirt, paddlers should paddle without a sprayskirt. This leaves us free to spend time learning some paddling terminology and to begin developing a sense of **teamwork**, as we will always paddle in the company of an experienced paddler, for safety reasons.

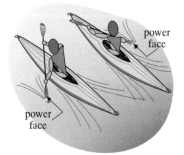

To better communicate when learning how to use the paddle, we will define the **power face** as the blade face that pushes against the water during the power stroke; the **reverse face**

Figure 37. Power face pushes water

is the other face. The concave side, or scoop side, of a curved blade is always that blade's power face.

When **using the paddle**, paddlers choose to use either **right-hand** or **left-hand control**. The **control-hand** holds firmly onto the grip while the **support-hand** allows the shaft to rotate freely.

Figure 38. Setting the grip - right hand control paddler

When **setting the grip** on the paddle relative to the control-hand's blade angle, we hold the shaft at a level between the chin and nose and grip the shaft such that the control-hand wrist is straight, its knuckles are parallel to the water, and the control-hand blade is perpendicular to the water. For a paddle with blades 90° offset, the support-hand blade will be parallel to the water's surface when setting the grip. The reason paddle blades are offset is to enable automatic **feathering**, or slicing, of the out-of-water blade through the air during each paddling stroke. *The instructors will be demonstrating paddle techniques using right-hand control.*

Now let's learn basic **control-hand/support-hand coordination**, which will answer the question, "what is each hand's function while paddling the kayak?" The general answer is that the control-hand always has a firm grip on the paddle shaft, and the support hand maintains a loose grip to enable the shaft to rotate, as determined by the control-hand. The best stroke to illustrate control-hand/support-hand coordination is the forward power stroke. To develop a better understanding, a paddler should step into the water up to his or her waist to simulate the feel of paddling without the complication involved by simultaneously having to control the kayak.

As we have already learned, the first step in performing the **forward power stroke,** or any stroke for that matter, is to set the blade angle relative to the control-hand. The next step in the forward power stroke is to take a stroke, starting with the control-hand blade. The blade starts in the water comfortably angled toward the bow, passes by the paddler's side, and ends when the blade emerges from the water and is parallel to the water's surface. At this point, the control-hand wrist is raised

Figure 39. Stroke drill right

27

up-and-back, and, again, the support-hand allows the shaft to rotate as a result of the control-hand's movement. Now, the support-hand blade is angled forward, arcs vertically through the water next to the paddler's side, and finishes when parallel to the water's surface. The control-hand will perform a natural recovery in preparation for the next stroke. If done correctly, the paddler standing in the water will feel a lot of resistance by the water during each half of the stroke.

Figure 40. Stroke drill left

This drill should continue for many strokes. Remember, Gary is demonstrating using right-hand control.

When performing the forward power stroke in the kayak, paddlers should concentrate on the "punch" or "push" of the hand on the out-of-water blade's grip; the punch should contribute about 80% of the force of the stroke. The paddler should concentrate on making the top "punch" arm hand end up directly over the center of the bow deck; frequently, the heel of the "punch" hand bumps the bow deck.

Shoulder rotation, which takes advantage of the large back muscles, contributes most

Figure 41. Punch forward

Figure 42. Rotate shoulders

of the "punch" energy. Shoulder and arm muscle energy will play a contributory role in the forward power stroke. The paddler's **shoulder rotation** should be smooth and natural; the torque, or twisting force, produced by the upper body and the shoulders translate to the paddle during each forward power stroke.

A paddler's **body position during paddling** can make paddling easier and more efficient. When paddling a kayak, paddlers must have complete body control over the kayak to make **paddling a straight course** possible. This means that the foot pedals are set such that the paddler's knees, hopefully protected by knee pads, are pressing firmly, yet comfortably, against the underside of the bow deck. To help in paddling a straight course, paddlers lean forward

Figure 43. Forward stroke right

Figure 44. Forward stroke left

when paddling the kayak in a forward direction. In addition, balancing the kayak to rest flat on the water will keep the kayak from turning when trying to paddle a straight course. Crossing one's punch arm across the center line of the kayak will tend to make the kayak turn. Also, the strokes on the port and starboard should be even in rhythm and length to help keep the kayak from turning. **Hull balance** is developed a little more each time one paddles. Remember - kayaking is a finesse sport where technique is more important than strength.

Figure 45. Practice following on a straight paddling course

The **reverse stroke** is approximately the reverse of the forward power stroke in arm and shoulder motion. We begin with the top hand over the center line of the kayak and pull with the top hand while pushing with the bottom hand. Paddlers should concentrate on the shoulder rotation and try to keep the strokes smooth and even.

The reverse stroke tends to be more strenuous due to the unnatural shoulder rotation and may need to be performed more slowly than a forward power stroke. Also, remember to lean backward when reverse paddling to lower the stern of the kayak in the water, which helps keep the kayak on a straight paddling course.

Figure 46. Reverse stroke

We should now be proficient in making the kayak go forward and backward, but we need to be able to *turn* the kayak to head back to shore. The strokes we will use to spin the kayak are called sweeps. Before learning sweeps, let's first understand the mechanics behind making the kayak spin.

pivot point

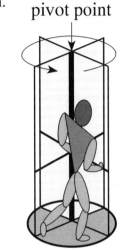

The **center of the kayak** is the center, or **pivot point**, about which the kayak spins. The farther away from the pivot point a force is placed on the kayak, the more effect the force will have in making the kayak spin. A good analogy is a **revolving glass door**. The door revolves more easily when pushed on farther away from where the doors meet in the center.

Figure 47. Revolving glass door analogy

In kayaking, with every *paddle action*, there is an equal and opposite *kayak reaction*. So, if we sweep, or arc our blade smoothly through the water in a clockwise direction, the kayak will spin counterclockwise. And, if we sweep our blade counterclockwise, the kayak will spin clockwise.

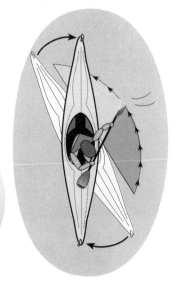

Figure 49. Forward sweep - wide reach

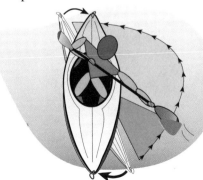

Figure 48. Forward sweep - start at bow

31

Based on the kayak spinning principle just discussed, the paddler should lean forward, when the blade is angled toward the bow, and lean back, when the blade is angled toward the stern, to put the blade (the force producing element) as far away from the pivot point as possible. Also, the blade should make a 180 degree arc because the paddler is seated directly over the pivot point, which means the entire sweep will contribute to the spin.

Now that we understand kayak spinning theory, let's understand making a kayak spin in practice. To begin a **forward sweep**, the paddler first sets the control-hand blade as if preparing for the power stroke. Now, instead of running the blade vertically through the water, the blade will sweep from bow to stern in a semicircular path. To create this motion, the outside arm is kept

Figure 50. Forward sweep start

Figure 51. Forward sweep 180° - finish at the stern

straight and the "punch" arm will be kept bent. The paddler's body will twist at the waist and the "punch" arm hand will cross the center line to the opposite side of the kayak because in the sweep, unlike the power stroke, the goal is to make the kayak spin. The paddler will want to lean into the turn, which is on the side opposite the paddle. To make the next forward sweep, simply raise the blade out of the water and begin again with that blade. Note that the power faces for the forward sweep stroke are the same sides as those during the forward power stroke.

In the **reverse sweep**, the reverse face will push the water as the blade travels from stern to bow in a semicircular path. The outside arm is kept nearly straight and inside arm is kept bent. As in the forward sweep, the main force will be created by the paddler's

Figure 52. Reverse sweep start

Figure 53. Reverse sweep 180° - finish at the bow

twisting at the waist. When the in-the-water blade reaches the bow, the blade will be lifted out of the water and set in the water behind the paddler in preparation for the next reverse sweep.

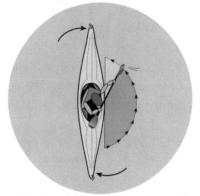

Figure 54. Combination spin - forward sweep

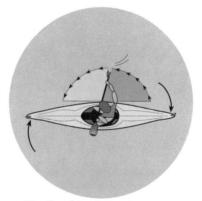

Figure 55. Combination spin -reverse sweep

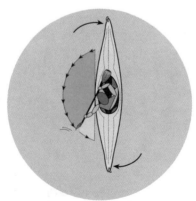

Figure 56. Combination spin - forward sweep, again

The paddler can spin the kayak to port and starboard using either forward or reverse sweeps. So, if the paddler wishes to spin the kayak to port using the forward sweep, the blade should be swept on starboard. The paddler can also spin the kayak to port or starboard using the reverse sweep on the side of the direction of spin. So, if the paddler wishes to spin the kayak to starboard using the reverse sweep, the blade should be swept on starboard.

Experienced paddlers save on recovery time by using a combination of the forward and reverse sweeps on alternating sides. To stop the spin, paddlers simply place the blade in the water in a sweep position and slowly reverse the blade sweep direction.

Now that we are familiar with the forward power stroke, the reverse stroke, and sweeps, let's concentrate on extended straight line paddling, because beginners often find their kayak turns when trying to paddle a straight line. Let's review some basics in achieving straight line paddling. Both feet should press with *equal pressure on the foot pedals* and both knees with *equal upward pressure on the hull*. Paddlers should *sit centered* in the seat to

Figure 57. Paddling practice

keep the kayak flat on the water and *lean in the direction of travel*. Punching directly to the bow tip and maintaining smooth and even length paddling strokes while keeping the *head up* and *eyes focused on the target* will prove beneficial in maintaining the straight course. Paddlers should be conscious that the blades pass through the water with the power faces perpendicular to the water being pushed. Finally, experienced paddlers who find the kayak starting to turn will add some wide power strokes or even forward sweeps to correct their paddling course. Diligent practice will undoubtedly result in straight line paddling proficiency.

Beginner Review

1. **Safety.** (a) Name as many recommended safety equipment items as you can. (b) Name some weather and water conditions that might make a paddler think twice before starting a day on the water.

2. **Kayak nomenclature.** Kayak nomenclature is a paddler's most important communication tool. List as many tangible and intangible parts of the kayak as you can.

3. **Paddle nomenclature.** Paddlers know the parts of a paddle by certain names. Can you recall and list the parts of a kayak paddle? (Hint: draw one to help you visualize).

4. **Choosing a paddle.** We learned three methods for choosing a white water paddle size. Can you describe one method?

5. **Portaging the kayak.** Paddlers portage, or carry, kayaks between storage areas and the water's edge. List three methods, each with one of its respective benefits.

6. **Entering/Exiting the kayak.** (a) Paddlers keep their knees straight and toes pointed to the bow when lowering themselves from the stern deck onto the seat. Why? (b) How do paddlers use the paddle to help keep the kayak stable and stationary while entering and upright-exiting the kayak?

7. **Wet exit.** Before ever paddling a kayak, Beginner Paddlers learn the wet exit procedure to prepare for an unexpected capsize. The wet exit drill is practiced in the presence of a spotter. (a) List the steps of a comfortable wet exit. (b) The most important idea to remember is "stay _____".

8. **Forward power stroke.** During the forward power stroke, paddlers rotate their shoulders and push the top hand directly to the bow so as not to cause the kayak to turn undesirably. What else might cause the kayak to turn undesirably?

9. **Sweeps.** When performing sweeps, we lean into the direction of the turn, keep our sweeping blade-side arm straight, push the other arm across the bow deck, and rotate at the hips to add power to the sweep. Why do we want the sweeping blade to be as far away from the kayak as possible?

10. **Straight line paddling.** River kayaks tend to turn when paddlers want to paddle on a straight course because of the flat hull. What tips would you give a Beginner Paddler to help him or her paddle on a straight course should he or she find the kayak constantly turns to starboard or port?

Exercise.
In the company of an experienced partner, paddle twenty forward power strokes, stop, then perform twenty reverse power strokes. Repeat until both forward and reverse directions can be performed in a straight line.

We're now one stroke along on The Kayak Express!

Intermediate Tools

- **kayak physical dimensions**
- **sprayskirt nomenclature**
- **putting on a sprayskirt**
- **attaching the sprayskirt**

Besides kayak nomenclature, we should also know some terms for the **physical dimensions** of our craft. The **length** of the kayak is simply the distance from the bow tip to the stern tip; generally, a shorter kayak is a more maneuverable kayak. The **beam** or **width** of the kayak refers to the widest part of the craft. The **weight** of a kayak is usually defined without paddler gear. **Rocker** is the banana shape of the boat; more rocker makes the kayak easier to turn. The **volume** refers to the amount of air space inside the kayak. Kayaks with more volume are more buoyant when sealed with a sprayskirt than are kayaks with less volume.

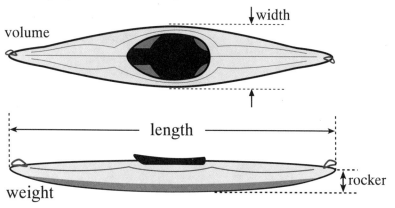

Figure 58. Kayak physical dimensions

In the Intermediate Section, we will discuss maneuvers that require the paddler to wear a **sprayskirt**, which makes a watertight seal around the cockpit coaming and keeps the kayak from filling with water. The sprayskirt, usually made of neoprene, nylon, or other waterproof material, is worn around the paddler's waist. The purpose of using the sprayskirt is to keep water out of the kayak, even if the paddler is upside-down. The sprayskirt has a **cockpit coaming seal ring** at its bottom outside that is usually created by shock cord inside the sprayskirt or may be wholly made of rubber. This seal ring is the part of the sprayskirt that attaches to the cockpit coaming to form a watertight seal. The top of the sprayskirt narrows to fit snugly around the paddler's waist, making a watertight seal; the narrow, top part of the sprayskirt is called the **waistband**. The **sprayskirt grabloop** is located on the top front of the sprayskirt and is used by the paddler to release the sprayskirt from the cockpit coaming.

When **putting on a sprayskirt**, the paddler holds the sprayskirt by the waistband with the grabloop on the top side of the sprayskirt directly in front of him or her, steps carefully into the waistband, and pulls the sprayskirt up until the bottom of the waistband is above the hips. The waistband of the sprayskirt should lay flat against the body of the paddler, which is important for keeping water from entering the kayak, as we shall learn during the rolling exercises.

Figure 59. Step into sprayskirt

Figure 60. Pull waistband up until flat

Attaching the sprayskirt to the cockpit coaming is an important skill because it is performed quite often. To attach the sprayskirt onto the cockpit coaming, we should set the back edge into position and lean on it to hold the sprayskirt's cockpit coaming seal ring in place.

Figure 61. Attach back of sprayskirt first

Next, we stretch the front edge of the cockpit coaming seal ring and guide it onto the bow edge of the cockpit coaming while still leaning back, against the sprayskirt. Ensure the sprayskirt grabloop is accessible to permit a rapid wet exit, if necessary.

Figure 62. Lean back and reach forward

The cockpit coaming seal ring attachment is finished by easing it onto the cockpit coaming's port and starboard side areas.

Figure 63. Complete sprayskirt fitting

The paddler will repeat the sprayskirt attachment process many times during the course of a paddling day. The steps of attaching the back, leaning on the back and reaching forward to connect the front, and securing the sides of the sprayskirt will always be repeated in this order. This ordered method of attaching the sprayskirt reduces the time it takes to seal the sprayskirt to the cockpit coaming and ensures that the sprayskirt is properly connected.

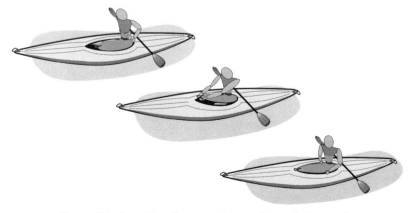

Figure 64. Attaching the sprayskirt to the cockpit coaming

Intermediate Practical

- spotter roll
- wet exit with sprayskirt
- Eskimo rescue
- deep water entry
- kayak-over-kayak rescue

In the Beginner Strokes section, we learned how to use a paddle, paddle a kayak forward and backward, and make it spin. In the Intermediate Strokes section, we will be learning strokes and braces that require us to balance the kayak on its side. To perform these balancing maneuvers, we will need to wear a sprayskirt to keep water from filling the kayak. Wearing a sprayskirt when paddling adds another step to the wet exit should a wet exit be necessary.

Before learning the wet exit with the sprayskirt, paddlers should be comfortable with their spotter and trust his or her ability to upright them in the kayak. To upright a capsized paddler, the spotter will use what we will call the spotter roll. To perform the **spotter roll**, the spotter reaches across the hull near the cockpit, places his or her hands on the bow or stern deck and leans back to use body weight to right the kayak.

Figure 65. Spotter reaches across hull

The paddler assists the spotter by holding onto the hull while leaning forward, which has the effect of reducing the amount of turning force the spotter must produce.

40

Figure 66. Spotter uses weight to roll paddler

The spotter roll is a technique by which the paddler does not need to wet exit, but all paddlers who wear sprayskirts when paddling must be prepared to unfasten the sprayskirt in the event a wet exit is necessary. Paddlers call this the **sprayskirt release**. The method for unfastening the sprayskirt from the cockpit coaming is to take hold of the grabloop, pull the grabloop forward, then pull it up. The sprayskirt release is to be added to the wet exit drill immediately after the "thumbs up" signal. Paddlers should practice the pull-out-and-up sprayskirt release in an upright position before performing it while overturned.

Figure 67. Sprayskirt release - pull the grabloop forward <u>then</u> up

Remaining calm is the most important part of any wet exit. To help us remain calm, we should consider that the wet exit, even with the sprayskirt release, can be done easily within the time we can hold our breath. A calm, wet exit with sprayskirt release is performed by: tucking forward, holding the kayak bottom when turning over, tapping three times, giving the thumbs up signal, pulling forward-then-up on the sprayskirt grabloop, keeping legs straight with toes pointed forward during the forward somersault. If the paddler is uncomfortable with any part of the wet exit with sprayskirt, he or she should repeated thump on the kayak to alert the spotter to perform the spotter roll. As with the first time we practiced the wet exit, we should execute three good wet exits with the sprayskirt before continuing. Each wet exit should become smoother and more relaxed.

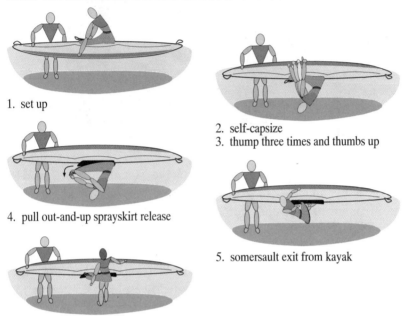

1. set up

2. self-capsize
3. thump three times and thumbs up

4. pull out-and-up sprayskirt release

5. somersault exit from kayak

6. wet exit complete

Figure 68.   Wet exit with sprayskirt

Both the spotter roll and the wet exit with sprayskirt rescue techniques have drawbacks when paddling in deep water, so good paddlers who work together as a team learn another method of rescue, the Eskimo rescue. The **Eskimo rescue** enables a capsized paddler to right the kayak with the aid of a spotter, but the spotter, in this Eskimo Rescue, will be in a kayak, rather than standing in the water. The Eskimo rescue saves a lot of time because the capsized paddler remains in the kayak, and, since the capsized paddler is wearing a sprayskirt, his or her need to drain the water from the kayak is removed.

The **Eskimo rescue drill procedure** is as follows.   First, the capsizing paddler places his paddle sufficiently far from his or her kayak and out of the spotter kayak's paddling approach path. Second, the two paddlers say the word "ready," one after the other. Third, the capsizing paddler self-capsizes and slowly slides his hands back and forth in search of the rescue craft bow.

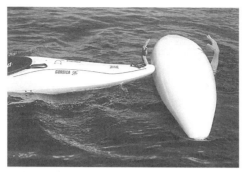

Figure 69. Eskimo rescue - slide hands back and forth

Fourth, the paddling spotter gently brings his or her bow to the midsection of the overturned kayak so the capsized paddler can gain hold of the rescue craft. Fifth, once the capsized paddler locates the rescue craft, he or she puts both hands on the rescue craft.

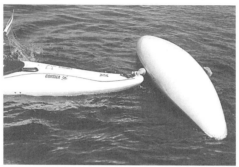

Figure 70. Eskimo rescue - take hold of the rescue craft's bow

The capsized paddler should use hips and legs to roll the kayak upright, *then* bring his or her head out of the water. A paddler attempting to bring his or her head up *before* rolling the kayak will find out what the term "muscling the kayak" means. Muscling the kayak may strain or injure the paddler's shoulder.

Figure 71. Eskimo rescue - keep head down and let the hips do the work

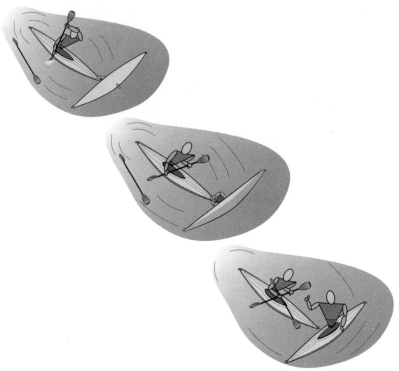

Figure 72. Eskimo Rescue sequence

On rare occasions, the paddler will want or need to enter a free-floating kayak. This maneuver is called a **deep water entry**, which requires some strength, patience, and a lot of balance. The re-entering paddler will reach fully across the kayak - often using the opposite side of the cockpit coaming as a grab point - and kick to get his or her torso onto the kayak. In a smooth motion, the paddler will then swing one leg over the kayak to straddle the stern deck with weight evenly distributed. Moving slowly, the paddler enters the kayak using the standard upright kayak entry. Moving both legs simultaneously helps to keep the kayak balanced. The paddler hand-paddles to the floating paddle and is underway.

Figure 73. Deep water entry - straddle method

Another method of deep water kayak entry is to do a **beam entry**. The beam entry requires the swimming paddler to be next to the cockpit when beginning the entry. The paddler will hold the cockpit coaming, pull him or herself up across the cockpit (using a strong kick if necessary) until the hips are directly above the cockpit, and roll onto his or her back such that the paddler is now sitting on the seat with legs dangling outside the cockpit on the side entered. The paddler will then slowly swivel him or herself to face the bow. Finally, the paddler will perform a standard upright entry by bringing the feet into the cockpit, pushing him or herself off the seat by pressing down on the stern deck with both hands, straightening legs and pointing toes forward, then sliding down to the seat.

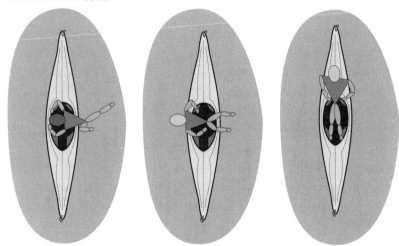

Figure 74. Deep water entry - beam method

Figure 75. Assisted deep water entry - beam method

We are now familiar with the Eskimo rescue, but sometimes our paddling partner is beyond the distance to assist in an Eskimo rescue. In this case, if a paddler must wet exit in deep water, the capsized paddler and the paddling partner can use the kayak-over-kayak rescue procedure to drain the capsized kayak.

Though the kayak-over-kayak rescue procedure is meant for deep water rescue, both paddlers should rehearse both the rescuer and capsized paddler roles in this drill in *shallow* water because the rescue craft does have the potential to capsize unless each paddler understands the teamwork.

When rehearsing the kayak-over-kayak rescue, paddlers should be familiar with a general predetermined procedure. The following **kayak-over-kayak rescue procedure** can be modified according to paddlers' needs. First, the rescue paddler should check the capsized paddler's physical condition. Second, the rescue paddler positions his or her kayak perpendicular to and at one end of the capsized kayak, such that the rescuer can take hold of the capsized kayak. Third, the capsized paddler assists the paddler by rolling the kayak such that the cockpit faces the water. Fourth, as the rescue paddler lifts the end of the overturned craft onto the rescue craft bow deck, the capsized paddler can either push down on the opposite end of the overturned craft or straddle the stern of the rescue kayak.

Figure 76. Pull kayak out

Figure 77. Pull kayak across

Fifth, the rescue paddler slowly draws the water-filled kayak cockpit-side down onto the rescue craft bow deck so that water can drain. During the draw-and-drain process, the capsized paddler straddles the stern of the rescue kayak to add stability for the rescue paddler. The capsized paddler also holds both paddles. Sixth, the rescue paddler flips the drained kayak upright, then sets it in the water and steadies the now-empty kayak to enable a safe deep water beam entry.

Figure 78. Hoist kayak to drain

Figure 79. Assist deep water entry

After the paddles are retrieved and the paddlers are underway, the capsized paddler can be checked for signs of hypothermia and medical attention should be sought, if necessary.

Figure 80. Attach sprayskirt

Figure 81. Paddle on!

The kayak-over-kayak rescue can be difficult for some paddlers, so we should remember that the kayak will float because of the flotation bags. And, because the kayak floats, it can be paddled to shore where it can be drained using standard techniques. Paddling a swamped kayak is termed the **swamped-kayak paddle**, and hand paddling a

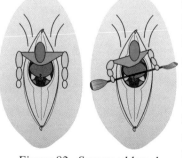

Figure 82. Swamped kayak swim and paddle

swamped kayak is the **swamped kayak swim**. The method of getting into the swamped kayak is the same as the deep water entry, except the kayak will be more stable. Paddlers should stay with a swamped kayak rather than swimming to shore, except in the case of an emergency, because *a kayak is much easier to spot than a lone swimmer.*

47

Intermediate Strokes

- moveable & sculling draw
- moveable pushaway
- stationary draw
- sideslipping
- hip snaps
- high brace
- low brace
- stationary pivot
- Duffek stroke & low brace turn

In the Beginner Strokes section, we learned strokes to move forward, backward, and spin. As Intermediate Paddlers, we will learn how to move a kayak sideways, angle the kayak on its side, and combine several strokes to turn the kayak while maintaining forward momentum. At the end of the Intermediate Strokes section, paddlers who have practiced diligently, always at their own pace, will have learned all the strokes necessary to paddle a Class 2 river in the company of an experienced river paddler.

Sometimes paddlers wish to move their kayaks directly sideways. In the Beginner Strokes section, we learned that moving the blade from bow to stern with the power face pushing the water results in making the kayak move forward. With that understanding, we can see that using the power face and pulling the water directly toward the side of the kayak will result in making the kayak move sideways. The **moveable draw** is the name of the stroke associated with the motion of moving the power face toward the kayak.

Figure 83. In-the-water recovery

Figure 84. Moveable draw

Mechanically, the paddler performs the moveable draw by setting the control hand grip as if performing the power stroke, but rather than putting the blade in the water near the bow, the blade is placed into the water as far to the side of the paddler as can be reached with the paddle remaining nearly vertical. The power face faces the kayak rather than the stern during the moveable draw. As in the forward power stroke, the control-hand is used to rotate the paddle shaft to angle the blade in the water, and the support-hand allows the shaft to rotate freely.

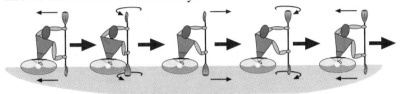

Figure 85. Moveable draw with an in-the-water recovery

Though the paddle is being drawn toward the kayak, the kayak is really moving *toward the paddle* being moved in the water. Remember, because the kayak moves in an equal and opposite reaction to paddle movement through the water, the kayak moves toward the paddle that is being drawn directly sideways through the water toward the kayak's hull. To assist in the moveable draw, experienced paddlers use their hips to slide the kayak toward the blade.

Once the blade is beside and parallel to the side of the kayak, the paddler has a choice of two moveable draw recovery methods for moving the paddle into position for the next stroke. The paddler can either raise the blade out of the water and place it back in the water away from the hull, known as the **out-of-water recovery**, or the paddler can rotate the blade such that the power face faces the stern to slice through the water, referred to as the in-the-water recovery. The **in-the-water recovery** is a little more difficult to learn than the out-of-water recovery, but it tends to be a quicker method of getting the blade set for the next stroke. Although rotating the control-hand up-and-back to angle the power face toward the kayak may feel awkward, it is correct to do so because the wrist has more strength when raised up-and-back than when rolled forward to support the blade against the force of the water.

When **performing the moveable draw**, the paddle must be moved through the water directly beside and in-line with the kayak's pivot point or some degree of spinning will be experienced. Remember, the paddler performing the moveable draw thinks of him or herself shifting the kayak to the blade using hip action. Experienced paddlers find that leaning slightly onto the paddle will add power to the moveable draw.

The **moveable pushaway** stroke is exactly opposite to the moveable draw. When **performing the moveable pushaway**, the paddler starts the blade beside the kayak and pushes the reverse face against the water directly away from the side of the kayak. Once again, the paddler can either perform an out-of-water recovery or in-the-water recovery to ready the blade for the next stroke.

Figure 86. Moveable pushaway   *Figure 87. In-the-water recovery*

Paddlers generally prefer to perform moveable draws more than moveable pushaways because the moveable draw tends to be easier. As good Intermediate Paddlers, we should start to understand that a moveable draw on starboard is the same as a moveable pushaway on port, and vice-versa. In the course of practicing the moveable draw and moveable pushaway strokes, paddlers should prove this concept to themselves.

As suggested in the Beginner Section, kayaking is a finesse sport. As good Intermediate paddlers, we should challenge ourselves to make all our strokes smooth and graceful. The **sculling draw** is a stroke that can make us look smooth and graceful while also adding efficiency to making the kayak move sideways.

To **perform the sculling draw**, we place the blade vertically in the water beside the kayak with the power face facing the kayak. Then, we slide the blade alongside the kayak such that the blade's leading edge is angled approximately 30° away from the kayak. This means that if the blade is sliding toward the bow, the bow blade edge is away from the kayak, and if the blade is sliding toward the stern, the stern blade edge is angled away from the kayak. One can think of the blade's motion during the sculling draw as 'spreading peanut butter on smooth bread'.

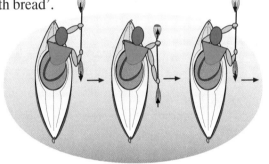

Figure 88. Sculling draw illustration

The term 'angled away from' simply means that one edge is farther from the kayak than the other edge. For example, as we slide the blade toward the bow, the leading blade edge is farther from the side of the kayak than the trailing blade edge.

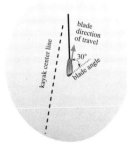

Figure 89. Sculling draw paddle angle

The sculling draw should be practiced on both sides of the kayak as we do with all our kayak paddling strokes. The more paddlers practice and master the sculling draw, the more they come to understand that the increase in efficiency over the moveable draw with recovery is due to never stopping the stroke.

We now know how to move a stationary kayak sideways, but we may wish to perform this action on a kayak which has forward momentum. The stroke we use to make a moving kayak sideslip is called a **stationary draw**. The stationary draw is related to its moveable counterpart in that the kayak will move toward the paddle when the stationary draw is applied. The difference between the moveable draw and the stationary draw is that the moveable draw requires paddler power whereas the stationary draw uses the power of the kayak's movement.

Let's take a detailed look at the blade position during the **stationary draw sideslip**. The blade is held nearly perpendicu-

Figure 90. Stationary draw sideslip

lar to the surface of the water with the leading edge angled outward at approximately 30°. The power face during the power stroke is the blade face that will be taking the force of the rushing water. The control-hand wrist is raised up and back to set the blade angle. The blade should be placed directly to the side of the kayak's pivot point. Paddlers learn where the kayak's pivot point is located when learning the art of the sideslipping a kayak because placing the blade in front of the kayak's pivot point will make the kayak turn, or pivot, toward the blade, and placing the blade behind the pivot point will make the kayak pivot away from the paddle. In addition, too much blade angle will have the effect of slowing or stopping the kayak, and too little blade angle will not have the desired sideslipping effect. As suggested

*Figure 91. Stationary draw
sideslip path*

earlier, paddlers must be conscious not to expose their shoulders, which is why, when performing the stationary draw stroke, the top arm's forearm is raised only as high as, and placed across, the paddler's forehead.

For the next set of strokes, we will need more refined body control over the kayak. To gain this skill, we practice what is called a "**hip snap**." What this means is that the hips, legs, and feet - which fit well in the kayak through adjustment of the foot braces - all work together to roll the kayak onto its side and then back onto its hull. The objective of practicing the hip snap is to develop our balance sensitivity and to develop a strong hip snap, which we will learn is one of the most important aspects of successful performance of the remaining strokes in this section as well as rolling the kayak.

When **practicing the hip snap**, paddlers can use a dock or floating raft where the water is deep enough for the paddler to perform a wet exit should the kayak accidentally capsize. If working at a dock, wearing a helmet is a good idea. Now let's watch Gary demonstrate the hip snap. First, he places the paddle on the dock. Next, he holds the dock as low to the water as possible, lays his head as much possible as on his brace-side shoulder, and slides the kayak away from the

Figure 92. Hip snaps - rock over   *Figure 93. Hip snaps - rock back*

dock. Gary then begins to rock the kayak back and forth - from its hull, to its side, then back onto the hull - allowing the kayak to come over his waist. The hip snap is quick and forceful and Gary's brace-side ear stays on his brace-side shoulder for the entire time.

Once confident with the hip snap on both sides, the paddler should advance to returning to a sitting upright position. While practicing going all the way back to a sitting upright position, paddlers give a good hip snap, keep the head on the brace-side shoulder until the kayak is upright, and concentrate on keeping pressure off their hands. Downward pressure of the hands is an indication the paddler is muscling the hip snap. The uprighting motion is all finesse; trying to muscle the kayak up will only make the paddler tired. As with the hip snap, paddlers should practice this uprighting motion on both sides until it becomes very easy and smooth.

Figure 94. Hip snaps - keep head on lean-to shoulder

Figure 95. Hip snaps - repeat rocking until confident

Figure 96. Hip snaps - reduce hands' downward force

Figure 97. Hip snaps - dip head and toss water

Once we have developed a good hip snap and righting motion, we are ready to practice the high brace. The **high brace** is used for preventing a capsize and is also used during the final stage of rolling the kayak.

Before beginning the high brace, *paddlers should be aware that a common, but infrequent, way of causing a shoulder injury or, potentially, a dislocation, is caused by applying pressure to the shoulder joints with one or both elbows raised above shoulder level.* Raising the arm too high is known as **exposing the shoulder**. The problem with shoulder dislocation is three-fold: first, the pain can be severe; second, the paddler could be overturned in the kayak with a dislocated shoulder; third, a person who has dislocated a shoulder once has a 60% chance of dislocating that shoulder again. For these reasons, we recommend keeping elbows low, warming up, and stretching the neck and shoulders to lessen injury risk.

As we watch Mark demonstrate the high brace, we should take note of several points. First, notice that the power face for the power stroke is pressing against the water during the high brace. Mark keeps his head cocked onto his shoulder on the high brace side until his hip snap is performed and the kayak is flat on the water's surface. A paddler who raises his or her head off the shoulder too early will raise his or her center of gravity, which will reduce his or her ability to perform a strong hip snap, resulting in a capsize. Another point of interest is that Mark places the blade on top of the water rather than slapping the

Figure 98. High brace - start easy

Figure 99. High brace - easy back

water. Finally, we observe that Mark tries to limit the amount of shoulder exposure by keeping his outstretched arm slightly bent and his inside arm's elbow near his body so that his shoulders are not exposed to injury or dislocation. After building confidence and finesse on both port and starboard, we should practice rocking back and forth lower and lower until we can toss water with our hair - just like the guys in sports videos.

Figure 100. High brace - progress lower

Figure 101. High brace - practice both sides until smooth

Paddlers who are planning to progress to the rolling exercises may wish to practice the high brace exercise while outfitted with a helmet and possibly even a wetsuit, because both pieces of gear will change a paddler's buoyancy, their feel for the water, and their ease of movement. The high brace is also frequently used while paddling on a river, where, we will learn, a helmet is a mandatory piece of equipment when kayaking. So, for the same reason the strokes are learned and practiced on flat water, paddlers should become familiar and comfortable with using white water gear on flat water.

Figure 102. High brace - paddler's point of view

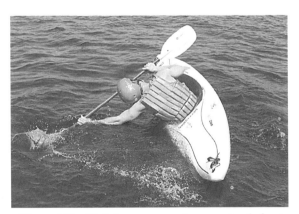

Figure 103. High brace - practice wearing helmet

As an alternative to the high brace, a **low brace** can be used to prevent the kayak from capsizing. When **performing the low brace**, the paddler uses the reverse blade face. As we can see from Mark's demonstration, the paddler's elbows are kept high when performing the low brace. In addition, Mark slides the blade forward along the water's surface by raising his control hand wrist up and back while at the same time using a hip snap to right the kayak. This blade motion aids the blade in staying at the water's

Figure 104. Low brace - roll blade across water toward bow

Figure 105. Low brace - practice both sides

surface. If performed well, paddlers will find the low brace to be a very powerful method for controlling unwanted kayak lean. Paddlers should practice rocking the kayak back and forth, performing the low brace on each side. Keeping the body loose and being fluid with the hip snap will make the low brace more effective and comfortable.

As Intermediate Paddlers, we should now be comfortable with the idea of rocking a kayak on its side, and safe in the knowledge that we have the tools - namely the high and low braces - to prevent an undesired capsize. Let's now take a break from the kayak rocking exercises and learn strokes that are used to make a moving kayak turn. The three strokes we shall learn are the stationary pivot, the Duffek stroke, and the low brace turn. Compared to the hip snap and high brace exercises these strokes will be relatively easy, but these turns are quite important on the river, so paddlers are encouraged to practice each stroke until it becomes effortless.

The first course-redirection stroke with which Intermediate Paddlers should familiarize themselves is the **stationary pivot**. The stationary pivot is exactly like the stationary draw sideslip, where the blade is held vertically in the water with its leading edge angled approximately 30° outward to the direction of travel, but for the stationary pivot, the paddler places the blade in front of the kayak's pivot point. The farther toward the bow the paddle is placed, the faster the kayak will spin.

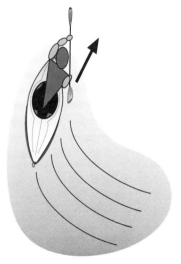

Figure 106. Stationary pivot

To practice the stationary pivot to starboard, paddlers paddle a straight course for several strokes, perform a forward sweep on port while leaning to starboard, then apply the stationary draw slightly ahead of their sitting position while maintaining the lean. As good Intermediate Paddlers, we practice the stationary pivot, as with all kayak strokes, on both port and starboard.

The next course-redirection stroke to learn is the Duffek stroke, which combines four strokes we have already learned into one fluid motion. The **Duffek stroke** is composed of the stationary draw, high brace, reverse sweep, and forward power stroke. Using the Duffek stroke, we can make a 90° turn in a moving kayak using little effort because we take advantage of the energy in the kayak's motion. In other words, we redirect the kayak without coming to a complete stop.

When practicing the Duffek stroke turn to starboard, the paddler paddles strongly in a straight line and performs a forward sweep on port while leaning to starboard to begin the turn. The paddler then places the stationary draw on starboard in front of him or her to keep the kayak turning, leans on a high brace to sharpen the turn, executes a reverse sweep with the blade toward the bow, and arcs the blade into a forward power stroke to come out of the 90 degree turn with some forward momentum. Experienced paddlers balance the kayak on the hull's side using leg and hip control to lean into the turn *as if riding a bicycle*. When practicing the Duffek stroke, we should notice that less high brace and reverse sweep results in less loss of forward momentum.

Figure 107. Duffek stroke - start with opposite side sweep

Figure 108. Duffek stroke - high brace into reverse sweep

Figure 109. Duffek stroke - finish with power stroke

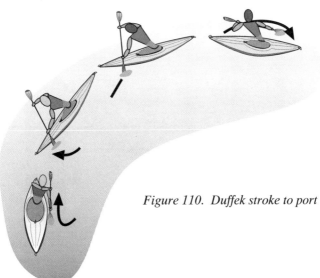

Figure 110. Duffek stroke to port

The last course-redirection stroke we will learn is the low brace turn. To perform the **low brace turn** to starboard, paddlers paddle a straight line for several strokes, make a forward sweep on port while leaning to starboard, then continue the lean on starboard as the starboard blade is placed flat onto the water's surface in a low brace position. The paddler's elbows are kept high during the low brace, just as when righting the kayak. Paddlers will come to understand after practicing the low brace stroke that the blade on the water's surface introduces drag that slows the kayak's forward momentum, but sharpens the turn. A paddler should determine if it is continued forward momentum or a quick turn that is important before executing the stationary draw turn. Gary is demonstrating a low brace turn that partially slows the kayak.

Figure 111. Low brace turn - start with opposite side sweep

Figure 112. Low brace turn - lean into turn

One way paddlers can improve their paddling skills is to design an **obstacle course** by using stationary buoys in the water, or simply by choosing other objects as markers. When paddling the obstacle course, paddlers should require the different strokes and turns introduced in the Beginner and Intermediate sections to be performed at different points along the course. Because paddlers can accidentally strike one another when paddling close together, and because a paddler's only competition is him or herself, the paddlers should start the course at great enough time intervals so as not to interfere with each other and should compete only against their own times. Each paddler should make three or more passes through the course, with ample rest in between, trying to reduce his or her time through the course. Time is a measure of efficiency, and efficiency is a measure of paddling finesse. The following skills are good to include in the obstacle course: forward power stroke, the reverse stroke, spins using sweeps, the moveable draw, the sculling draw, the low brace turn, the stationary pivot, and the Duffek stroke. Paddlers should run the course both clockwise and counterclockwise to improve both starboard and port paddling strokes.

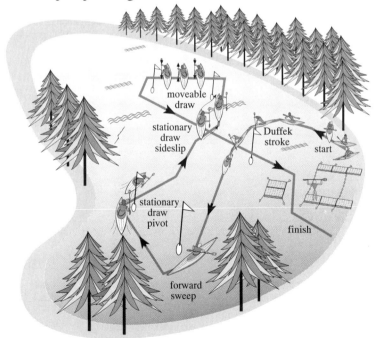

Figure 113. Obstacle courses should include many different skills

Intermediate Review

1. **Physical dimensions**. Knowing a kayak's physical dimensions helps paddlers determine whether or not to choose the kayak for a given set of water conditions. Name some kayak physical dimensions.

2. **Spray skirt nomenclature**. (a) The sprayskirt fits snugly around the paddler's waist and the _____. (b) The sprayskirt is worn high on the waist such that its _____ is in front of the paddler in case a wet exit is necessary.

3. **Wet exit with sprayskirt**. A wet exit with sprayskirt requires the paddler to release the sprayskirt from the cockpit coaming to enable the paddler to exit the cockpit. To release the sprayskirt, paddlers pull the sprayskirt's grabloop _____ and _____, in that order. (fill in the blanks).

4. **Eskimo Rescue**. The Eskimo rescue can be used by paddlers to upright a capsized kayak. (a) How many kayaks are involved in an Eskimo rescue? (b) Write a short Eskimo rescue procedure.

5. **Kayak-over-kayak rescue**. During the kayak-over-kayak rescue, the capsized paddler goes to the stern of the rescue paddler's kayak after the rescue paddler hoists one end of the capsized kayak onto the bow deck. What does the capsized paddler do at the stern of the rescuer kayak and why?

6. **Moveable draw**. The moveable draw is used to draw the kayak toward the blade in the water. What version of the moveable draw does not use a recovery between each stroke? (Hint: Like "spreading peanut butter on soft bread.")

7. **Hip snaps**. The goal of the 'hip snaps' exercises is to help paddlers reduce the downward force exerted by their hands and arms. With practice, paddlers will learn to rock the kayak using mainly their hips. While practicing hip snaps on port, a paddler's head should rest on the (left/right) shoulder. (choose the correct answer)

8. **High brace**. During the high brace, which blade face - the power face or reverse power face - presses against the water?

9. **Low brace**. The low brace is used as a quick response to prevent a kayak from leaning and possibly capsizing. When pressing against the water with he reverse power face and sliding the blade along the water's surface toward the bow, the paddler's elbows are kept (low/high). (choose the correct answer)

10. **Duffek stroke**. The Duffek stroke combines the stationary draw, high brace, reverse sweep, and forward power stroke into one fluid motion. (a) What stroke does an experienced Intermediate Paddler perform to start a Duffek turn to starboard? (b) On which of the four Duffek stroke parts does the paddler lean when angling the kayak on its side?

Exercise 1.
Perform the high brace back and forth without capsizing until you can get your hair wet on both starboard and port.

Exercise 2.
Balance the kayak on its side by sliding the blade with a climbing angle slowly back and forth.

We're now one more stroke along on The Kayak Express!

Advanced Tools

- **kayak materials**
- **kayak types**
- **kayak and paddle characteristics**
- **storing equipment**

As paddlers become more involved in the sport of kayaking, they invariably develop a need to have their own craft. As good paddlers, we should be educated in the different **styles of kayaks** available before committing to a purchase, because a well constructed craft can last a long time and we wouldn't want our skill potential to be limited by the craft. First, let's discuss some materials of which kayaks are made.

Many kayaks are generally made of plastic (usually polyethylene), fiberglass, or kevlar. Plastic kayaks are rugged and can be relatively inexpensive. Fiberglass kayaks tend to be lighter and more easily moved on the water than plastic kayaks. Kevlar kayaks are strong and light, but are more expensive than either plastic or fiberglass kayaks.

Figure 114. Kayak types - white water and touring craft

Kayaks and paddles come in many shapes, sizes, and styles. Similar kayak designs of each style can be found for both lighter and heavier paddlers. Some **kayak characteristics** a paddler may want to consider are acceleration, stability, surfing capability, rocker, storage, cockpit size, volume, and depth. Some features in paddle designs a paddler may want to consider are blade shape, blade size, blade material, shaft material and shape, weight, length, one or two pieces, and blade offset angle.

Two other popular kayak types are the touring kayak and the open-cockpit kayak. The touring kayak is used for paddling long distances. It is long, slender, well-balanced, and has foot-pedals that control a rudder, which is located at the stern. Open-cockpit kayaks do not accept a sprayskirt, making them appropriate beginners' craft because the paddling strokes can be practiced with little potential for mishap.

Figure 115. Canoe and kayak storage racks

Paddlers who own multiple craft should consider constructing a simple, sturdy, wooden rack system to store kayaks and canoes when not in use. Many paddlers place carpeting or other material over the wooden rails on which the craft will rest. At the time of this rack system construction, paddlers may also wish to consider hanging a clothes line in a sunny area to allow clothing to dry immediately after use.

Figure 116. Dry clothing and gear after use

Advanced Practical

- **square knot**
- **sheet bend**
- **bowline**
- **artificial respiration**

Paddlers often find the ability to tie **knots** to be useful during a day on the water. As good Advanced paddlers, we should be proficient in tying some simple knots. Three knots often used in the sport of kayaking are the square knot, the sheet bend, and the bowline.

Before we begin learning knots, we should familiarize ourselves with knot-tying nomenclature. A **rope** that has been cut for a specific purpose is called a **line**. When used for tying knots and hitches, a piece of line has two ends: a **standing end**, which remains fixed, and a **running end**, which will be moving in our hands.

Right over left, then left over right makes the **square knot**. The square knot can be used to make grab loops at the kayak's bow and stern.

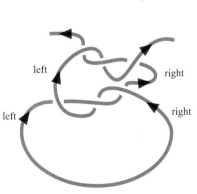

Figure 117. Square knot illustration

Figure 118. Completed square knot

If we want to connect two different pieces of line, we should use the square knot's cousin, the **sheet bend**. We start the sheet bend by making a loop in one of the lines. Then, the running end of the second line comes up through the loop, wraps around the first line, and is weaved between the loop and the standing end of the second line. One useful application of the sheet bend is to extend a heaving line.

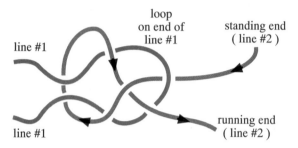

Figure 119. Sheet bend illustration

Figure 120. Completed sheet bend

The **bowline** is used for making a temporary loop at the end of a line for uses such as a temporary dock line. To tie a bowline, one twists an overhand loop with the running end thumb and forefinger. Then, with the running end, "the rabbit comes out of the hole, goes around the tree, and jumps back into the hole."

Figure 121. Bowline illustration

standing end

running end

Figure 122. Completed bowline

Knowledge of **artificial respiration** is important in kayaking because of the potential danger associated with the sport. As always, be prepared by knowing Red Cross standards, learning current medical artificial respiration techniques, and using common sense. A spotter would use artificial respiration on a victim paddler, or a swimmer, for that matter, in the event the victim were rescued from drowning and found not to be breathing. Artificial respiration should be continued until trained medical help arrives; it can be the saving difference.

Figure 123. Artificial Respiration discussion

Advanced Strokes

- screw roll
- Eskimo roll
- board roll
- frisbee roll
- hand roll
- river simulation

In the Intermediate Strokes section, we learned how to rock a kayak to its side then return it to its upright position by successfully using the high brace in conjunction with a strong, quick hip snap. Depending on our natural athletic abilities and practicing diligence, we may even have rocked the kayak enough to dip our heads and toss some water with our hair. Though the high brace head dip is a measure of one's progress, paddlers can still begin the rolling exercises if not yet at water level in the high brace exercise.

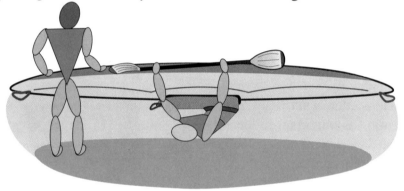

Figure 124. Upside-down position - preparing to roll

Rolling a kayak is defined as the act of uprighting an upside-down kayak while remaining in the kayak. For our purposes, we use the term "rolling" to mean "screw rolling," which is a rolling technique that keeps both hands in the standard grip position on the paddle shaft.

Fundamentally, the screw roll is an extension of the high brace. As we will learn when performing a roll, the paddler will need a good hip snap, fluid high brace, and discipline in keeping the brace-side ear on its shoulder until the kayak is upright again on the water. Besides the body motion skills, rolling the kayak combines skills and techniques we have already learned, namely capsizing the kayak, blowing air out of the nasal passages when upside-down, remaining calm, trusting the spotter, and working as a team with the spotter.

Since paddlers always work as partners (never alone) in the rolling exercises drills, the spotter will be standing next to the kayak in a paddler's early rolling development. Later, when a paddler has learned to roll and continues practicing until the roll becomes as natural as the Duffek stroke, the spotter will watch from another kayak, ready to assist with an Eskimo Rescue in the event the paddler is unsuccessful in the roll. Working in a flat water confined environment allows for either of these spotter rescue techniques. In cases where we are unsuccessful in rolling the kayak and a rescue craft is too far from the overturned craft, we may have to remember our humble beginnings and revert to using the wet exit technique.

Let's start the **rolling exercise** by breaking down the rolling exercise into four component parts: rolling set up, inverted position, uprighting set up, and uprighting combination. We **will**

Figure 125. Screw roll component parts (right-side high brace)

study each step in general terms, so they are applicable to left or right side paddlers, that is, paddlers who like to complete the roll with the left or right side blade. So, paddlers who find the high brace easier to one side may want to begin learning the roll such that the high brace part of the roll is performed on the favored side.

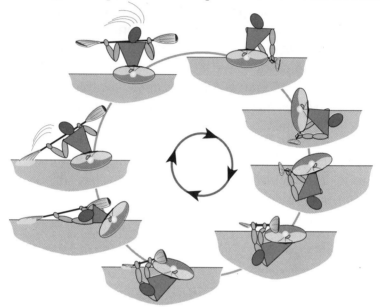

Figure 126. Screw roll component parts (left-side roll)

However, paddlers should not shy from learning to roll on both sides, even though most paddlers eventually settle on rolling to one side or the other, which is perfectly fine for most situations.

Paddlers begin the **rolling set up** by going through a **checklist of questions**: Is the water sufficiently deep to ensure my head will be clear of the water's bottom while upside down? Are the foot pedals properly positioned against the hull to yield a high degree of body control over the kayak? Am I comfortable with the wet exit with sprayskirt in case bailing out becomes necessary? Am I working with someone experienced enough either to roll my inverted kayak with me in it or to assist in an Eskimo rescue?

After answering "yes" to all of the suggested rolling set up preliminary questions, we can go on to the next part of the rolling set up, which is **paddle placement**. The paddler places the paddle shaft alongside the kayak and below the water's surface. The blade closer to the bow should be set parallel to the water's surface such that its power face faces the paddler. Note that the control-hand maintains its standard grip, where the control-hand wrist is rotated up-and-back, if necessary, to turn the power face toward the paddler. For example, when setting up for a roll on starboard, a right-hand control paddler will place the right blade's power face forward and parallel to the water's surface by keeping the right wrist straight. When setting up for a roll on port, a right-hand control paddler will place the left blade's power face forward and parallel to the water's surface by raising the right wrist up-and-back.

Gary is demonstrating the paddle position before self-capsizing. He tucks his chin, places his ear on his high brace side shoulder, and sets his high brace blade angle. The high brace blade during the rolling set up is the blade beside the kayak closer to the bow. We should

Figure 127. Screw roll - assist set up   *Figure 128. Screw roll - guide paddle*

notice that placing one's hands and paddle *underwater* in the rolling set up results in the paddle being high out of the water in the inverted position, which is of critical importance for moving the blade to the uprighting set up position.

While in the inverted position, the paddler remains tucked forward, continuously but conservatively blows air through his nose, and holds his position until he feels the air cool his wet hands. When the paddle is fully in the air, the spotter assists the paddler by guiding the

Figure 129. Screw roll practice - supporting the blade

paddler's blade to the uprighting set up position. In the paddler's early rolling development, the spotter should assist by holding the high brace blade neck and sweeping the blade out to the uprighting set up position. The spotter will want to position him or herself between the kayak and the sweeping blade so as not to get struck by the blade.

As the paddler learns through repetition how the body must move to place the blade in the uprighting set up position, the spotter can yield control to the paddler by supporting the paddle by the blade rather than by the neck. The key to a paddler's **successful roll development** begins by his or her developing a feel for keeping the sweeping blade

Figure 130. Screw roll practice - assist during uprighting combination

on or above the water's surface while moving between the inverted position and the uprighting set up position. If the blade 'dives', the paddler will have difficulty in setting up for the high brace. After the paddler has developed a feel for getting the paddle perpendicular to the kayak with the blade at the water's surface, the spotter can wait to support the blade, lending a hand or two just as the paddler begins the high brace.

The rolling **uprighting combination** is used by paddlers to upright a capsized kayak without exiting the kayak. The uprighting combination combines a high brace with an effective hip snap. The reason we worked with our spotters during the hip snap exercises to reduce downward hand pressure was to prepare us for the uprighting combination, so now the hip snap should effectively perform most of the work when making the kayak roll.

Figure 131. Screw roll - blade set up

Now that we have learned the four parts of the screw roll, our next exercise is to begin rolling without the spotter's physical support. Paddlers performing the screw roll without the assistance of the spotter helping to guide the blade to the uprighting set up position have a choice for getting the blade in position to perform the uprighting combination. The upside down paddler may swing the blade totally in the air between the inverted and uprighting set up positions, which is a sign of experience, or the paddler can sweep the blade on the water's surface by angling the blade such that it has a climbing angle. To create the blade's climbing angle, the paddler will cock the control-hand wrist slightly forward after setting the power face during the rolling set up. The paddler will know the blade angle

75

is, in fact, a climbing angle through experience and feel (i.e., the blade does not dive into the water during the sweep). A paddler having doubt about whether the blade has a climbing angle on the water's

Figure 132. Feeling the blade angle

surface (so as not to have the blade dive when attempting to upright) can simply reach out and feel the blade's angle. Checking the blade angle is usually only necessary early in rolling development when beginning the uprighting combination without the spotter's assistance.

*Figure 133. Screw roll - allow
hands to surface*

*Figure 134. Screw roll - successful
roll under spotter's watch*

In the upside-down position, the paddler can sense his paddle blades are above the water's surface by the cool air felt on the hands. Paddlers who wait patiently until their hands have surfaced before beginning to swing or sweep their paddle to the uprighting set up position tend to be successful in their rolling attempts. Also, paddlers conserve energy by waiting for the blade to surface because sweeping a submerged blade requires excess energy.

Figure 135. Screw roll - spotter ready for Eskimo rescue

We should begin to understand that the uprighting set up position is actually the high brace arm position, combined with being beneath the kayak. And, as in the high brace, the brace-side blade's power face will be pressing against the surface of the water. The uprighting set up position starts us in a high brace position: head on the brace-side shoulder, outer arm outstretched, and power face flat on the water's surface. Finally, a fluid hip snap, finished with a head flick to toss water, completes the roll.

Figure 136. Screw roll - self-capsize

Figure 137. Screw roll - get way back

Some tips in performing a successful screw roll are the following:

1. Ensure the kayak "fits" well; one's feet should be firmly against the foot pedals with knees pushing against the inside of the bow deck.

2. Start the high brace with the brace-side blade angled behind the paddler's seat position.

3. Concentrate on starting the uprighting combination with the blade flat on the water's surface.

4. The hip snap should be quick and strong, such that very little force is put onto the high brace paddle blade; "muscling" the hip snap will cause the blade to submerge, making the uprighting combination strenuous and difficult to perform.

5. The paddler's brace-side ear should be against the brace-side shoulder until the kayak has successfully been uprighted. An experienced paddler will recognize that his or her brace-side ear does not stay against the brace-side shoulder in strenuous or even unsuccessful rolling attempts. Lifting the head causes the upper body to get ahead of the hip snap in the uprighting combination and causes the center of gravity to be too far over the side of the kayak. The high center of gravity creates a downward force on the high brace support blade which forces the blade beneath the water's surface, leading to a failed rolling attempt. Keeping the brace-side ear on the brace-side shoulder maintains a low center of gravity making the hip snap easier and requiring less force on the high brace support blade.

6. Arch the back during the uprighting combination to keep the center of gravity close to the kayak, which can practically guarantee a successful roll every time. A paddler will feel his or her PFD rub the stern deck when the body arch is done properly.

Figure 138. Screw roll - set up

Figure 139. Screw roll - high brace

Figure 140. Screw roll - hip snap

Figure 141. Screw roll - success!

The **Eskimo roll** can aid those who find themselves having a difficult time with the body motion when developing the screw roll. To perform the Eskimo roll, one slides both hands along the paddle until the brace-side hand is in the center of the shaft and the other hand is on the blade's tip and edge. The brace-side blade, being extended so far from the kayak, yields a large mechanical advantage, which makes rolling easier. The exact same body motion should be used as described for the screw roll.

Figure 142. Eskimo roll adds mechanical advantage

The paddler can use the Eskimo roll to help develop the mechanical skills necessary to roll the kayak. However, since the Eskimo roll requires paddlers to release their grip on the shaft, although only for an instant, this rolling technique is less favorable on rivers than the screw roll. For this reason, we recommend that paddlers developing their rolling skills should concentrate on the screw roll.

After the paddler can successfully perform a screw roll on at least one side, the paddler can challenge him or herself by reducing the mechanical advantage over the kayak. Mechanical advantage over the kayak is gained through use of the paddle; the farther the brace blade is placed from the kayak's center of rolling rotation, the more easily a paddler can roll the kayak. For instance, the Eskimo roll provides more mechanical advantage over the kayak than the screw roll.

Reducing the mechanical advantage can be done by discarding the paddle and using a flutter board (also known as a swimmer's kick board), then a frisbee, and finally, only the cupped hands. Notice that we are progressing from objects having large buoyancy, stiffness, and surface area to just the surface area our own cupped hands can provide. Other objects, such as a small rectangle of wood or even a PFD can be used as rolling devices during this exercise.

One will find that the hip snap technique will need to be very strong at the point of doing a hand roll. Besides an improved hip snap, other benefits from attempting the hand roll exercise will be the paddler's improved high brace and hip snap coordination and overall rolling confidence. This learning process, as in all paddling exercises and expeditions, must be conducted in the presence of an experienced paddler.

A flutter board is an ideal starter tool toward the development of the hand roll because it is extremely buoyant with a large surface area. Using a very buoyant object, like the flutter board, helps novice hand roll paddlers find the water's surface, which is initially a strange feeling without the paddle. In addition to aiding the paddler's hands in finding the water's surface, a highly buoyant object, like a flutter board, behaves in a way similar to a spotter's kayak during an Eskimo rescue.

When performing the **flutter board roll**, the rolling paddler goes through the same checklist of questions as during the rolling set up with the paddle. During the self-capsize, the paddler can choose

Figure 143. Flutter board roll set up

to position the flutter board for immediate rolling, or the paddler can choose to rotate his or her waist and flutter board after reaching the inverted position. The uprighting set up position is simply defined as having the left arm to stern if rolling to port, or

Figure 144. Flutter board roll - rotate board into position

right arm to stern if rolling to starboard. Also, the paddler should consider placing both hands on top of the flutter board to simulate the hand roll hand position and to prevent straining the wrist by holding the board's edge during the roll.

The flutter board uprighting combination includes the high brace with a strong, quick hip snap, just as rehearsed during the screw roll exercises. And, even more important than when performing the screw roll, paddlers need to keep the head down on the stern-

Figure 145. Flutter board roll - hip snap as usual

Figure 146. Flutter board roll - practice several

side shoulder during the flutter board roll to keep the center of gravity close to the kayak and to help the hip snap turn the kayak onto the hull. Fluidity during the flutter board roll plays a large part in a paddler's success.

After building some confidence with the flutter board roll, paddlers should discard the flutter board for a less buoyant, less stiff, and reduced surface area object, such as a frisbee. This roll is known as the **frisbee roll**. All the previous steps are the same, including placement of hands on top of the frisbee. Paddlers will find that a stronger and quicker hip snap will be necessary to provide sufficient righting energy. By the end of the frisbee roll drill, paddlers should be less dependent on their hands and arms and focus on the body motion.

Figure 147. Frisbee roll - think through procedure

The last rolling exercise we will be discussing is the **hand roll**. To perform a successful hand roll, the paddler is required to coordinate all parts of the roll into one quick, smooth motion. Some paddlers like to keep their thumbs interlocked, with hands cupped, other paddlers prefer a double water slap method where one arm will lead the other through the water's surface, and there are the rare expert paddlers who dazzle others by tucking their hands into

Figure 148. Hand roll - set up with cupped hands

their vests, relying solely on their ability to sweep their bodies far back onto the stern deck in conjunction with a well-timed hip snap to complete the roll. The message is that paddlers can develop their own hand roll styles to complement their individual strengths, but some traits common to all successful rolls will include a good hip snap, keeping the head down until the kayak has rolled or even arching back onto the stern deck to keep the center of gravity closer to the center of kayak rotation, and, of course, finesse.

Figure 149. Hand roll - strong, quick hip snap

Another view of the hand roll shows that keeping the head on the shoulder and executing a strong hip snap maintains a low center of gravity, allowing the paddler to more easily roll the kayak.

Figure 150. Hand roll - hands above surface to begin

Figure 151. Hand roll - very strong, quick hip snap

Figure 152. Hand roll - success!

85

After having fun waterlogging our heads while learning the hand roll, we should come back to the screw roll to see if we have improved our style and to practice some other rolling drills that we may find of use during a journey down a river.

The first and easiest rolling drill is to roll to starboard if uprighting on starboard rather than rolling to port and making a full revolution. This drill is not meant to be difficult - just different. Another rolling drill paddlers can try is holding the paddle with only one hand during the self-capsize.

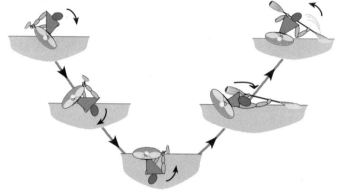

Figure 153. Same side roll drill

Yet another drill paddlers can try is to lay the paddle across the bow deck during the self-capsize. This paddle arrangement will have the effect of slowing the self-capsize to that which is often encountered during an accidental capsize on the river.

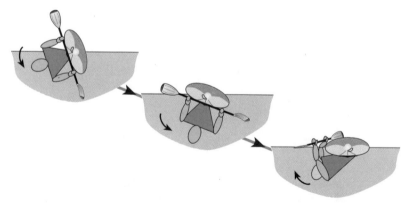

Figure 154. Paddle held across bow deck to simulate river capsize

The last of our rolling exercises, the **river capsizing simulation**, is performed by self-capsizing while paddling on a full speed, straight course. We should notice the sound the water makes as our heads enter the seemingly-moving stationary water.

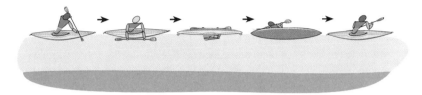

Figure 155. River simulation - paddle forward, self capsize, roll and go

In all the above advanced screw roll exercises, paddlers should stick with the fundamental paddling philosophies: learn and practice at a comfortable pace, practice in the company of an experienced paddler, and, of course, safety first.

We should also be aware that flat water rolling drills cannot fully prepare a paddler for rolling in moving water. For this reason, before beginning the day's river journey, experienced river paddlers adequately stretch and roll a few times in calm river water to build some confidence . If rolling on the river becomes necessary, we should relax and apply all we practiced together here in the Advanced Strokes section.

Figure 156. Screw roll - practice, practice, practice

Advanced Review

1. **Kayak materials**. Fiberglass kayaks are generally lighter than plastic kayaks. What advantage does a plastic kayak material have over a fiberglass kayak?

2. **Kayak types**. River kayaks are generally shorter than touring kayaks. (a) What main advantage does a shorter kayak offer a river paddler? (b) List three kayak characteristics that a paddler would want to know before choosing one for a specific purpose.

3. **Square knot**. The square knot can be used to tie gear inside the kayak. Either write the procedure outlined in the Advanced Practical section for tying a square knot or tie one.

4. **Sheet bend**. (a) Why is a sheet bend used? (b) Tie a sheet bend.

5. **Bowline**. (a) The bowline is used for making a (temporary/permanent) loop at the end of a line (choose the correct answer). (b) Tie a bowline.

6. **Screw roll 1**. In the Advanced Strokes section, we defined the screw roll to be composed of four parts. List them.

7. **Screw roll 2**. (a) What stroke from the Intermediate Strokes section is used during the uprighting combination of the screw roll? (b) During which part of the screw roll is the hip snap used?

8. **Eskimo roll**. While performing an Eskimo roll, the paddler holds the shaft with the roll-side hand and holds the tip of the other blade with the other hand. (a) What does this modified grip of the paddle do to the distance from the kayak of the roll-side blade? (b) How does this distance affect a paddler's ability to roll and why?

9. **Hand roll**. List some of the important points a paddler should keep in mind when learning the hand roll.

10. **River simulation**. Several variations of self-capsizing were suggested to get paddlers used to unexpected capsizing orientations. What makes the river simulation self-capsize different from the others?

Exercise 1.
Perform three rolls in a row on your strong rolling side.

Exercise 2.
Perform three rolls in a row on your less strong rolling side.

We're one stroke from completing The Kayak Express!

River Paddler Tools

• river gear

Running a river can be a thrilling experience, but a river is no place to kayak without proper safety equipment. This means that we should have on hand all the equipment recommended for flat water paddling.

Figure 157. River safety equipment

We also recommend additional **safety equipment specific to river paddling**, including: a bag-type heaving line (containing soft thick line), an extra paddle (the type that separates into two parts, to be easily stowed in the kayak), and duct tape for making quick temporary repairs to the kayak.

Figure 158. Duct tape

The **bag type heaving line** is used to rescue a paddler who is undesirably floating in the river. It is essential, therefore, that the line is, and remains, untangled so as to fully extend to the floating paddler. When packing the bag, the line should be randomly stuffed rather than coiled. Once the line is fully inside, we should make a practice throw to be certain that our individual stuffing methods do, in fact, perform as intended. Notice that the weight of the line in the heaving line bag

Figure 159. Bag-type heaving line

reduces as the line comes out during the heaving line bag's flight.

In addition to river kayaking safety equipment, paddlers should also be prepared with appropriate river clothing. The basic rule-of-thumb is for the mandatory use of either a wetsuit or drysuit is when the sum of the air and water temperatures is less than 100° F (38° C). A **wetsuit** allows a thin film of water to enter between the wetsuit material, often 1/8" thick neoprene for paddling, and

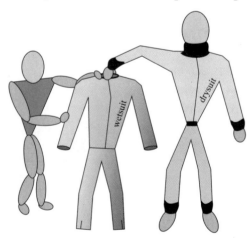

Figure 160. Wetsuit and drysuit

the paddler's skin. The thin film of water then heats up to body temperature, which keeps the paddler warm. A **drysuit** uses rubber cuffs that form a water tight seal at the neck, wrists, and ankles, and the body of the suit is made of a waterproof material. A drysuit allows paddlers to wear comfortable, warm clothing beneath it. Our PFD's should protect our entire upper bodies, including the back, and should be comfortable for long periods of paddling.

Figure 161. Inserting flotation bags

Figure 162. Inflating flotation bags

River Paddlers should make final checks and preparations of the kayak's internal equipment prior to starting on the river. Flotation bags should be installed in the kayak's bow and stern while not inflated, then inflated through the fill tube, just as we did in the Beginner section. After closing the flotation bag fill tube valve, paddlers should check that no flotation bag is losing air and that the fill tubes are carefully tucked away to avoid interference with feet and legs.

Depending on the strength of the river's current and our familiarity with the river, we may wish to include a helmet as a piece of our standard **white water river gear**. Of course, we always wear proper footwear while river paddling. River paddling requires plenty of energy, so bringing food in waterproof containers is a good idea. A hot or cold drink may also be appreciated.

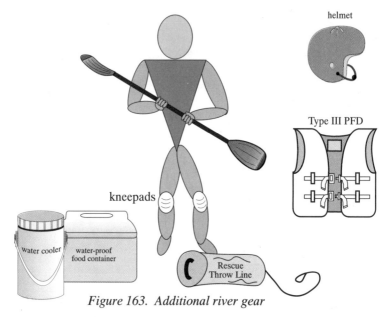

Figure 163. Additional river gear

Figure 164. River readiness discussion

Remember to tie all this gear securely to the kayak if taking it along. We should accept the potential for an unexpected capsize and be prepared accordingly.

River Paddler Practical

- selecting the river
- transporting the kayak
- knots
- reading the river
- scouting the river
- river obstructions
- universal signals
- river capsizing
- swimming the river

Figure 165. Selecting the river (class 1)

Selection of a river to paddle should be based on the paddlers' skill and experience as river paddlers. **Rivers are classified** from one to six for kayaks, where class 6 is the most difficult. (see River Classification Chart, page 147) We suggest rivers of Class 1 or 2 after developing proficient kayak handling skills, and Class 3 when experienced. Be aware that rivers tend to flow much faster in times of runoff, as in springtime. Call ahead for **seasonal information** about rivers you may wish to explore.

Figure 166. Selecting the river (class 3)

Figure 167. River water flow control dam

Hydroelectric **dams** are used to convert water flow energy into electric power. Because power is generated at a controlled rate by controlling the flow of water through a hydroelectric dam, paddlers often take advantage of the controlled water flow downstream of such dams in summer months, when many non-dam-controlled rivers are too low to paddle. The rate of water flow can be measured by **water markers** below the dam, where the height of water, as measured by the calibrated markings on the water marker, indicates the rate of water flow in the river. Although the rate of flow is controlled, heavy

Figure 168. River flow marker -
3100 cubic feet per sec

Figure 169. River flow marker -
6660 cubic feet per sec

rains can force the hydroelectric dam operators to open flood gates, potentially causing river flow to vary by several thousand cubic feet per second from one week to the next.

After selecting the river, we may need to **transport a kayak** to it, so a river team should know how to **secure a kayak** to the roof of a car. We begin by centering the kayak on a sturdy set of roof racks. The hull should be secured in place using **bungee cord** or straps specially designed for the **car rack system**.

Figure 170. Strapping down the kayak

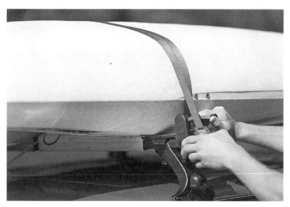

Figure 171. Cranking down the straps

With strong line, such as 1/2" nylon or dacron, the kayak's bow and stern grabloops can be tied directly to the car frame. We may also wish to tie another contact point to the rack using several wraps of line and an appropriate hitch or knot. Be overcautious - nothing is worse than seeing your kayak follow you down the interstate highway.

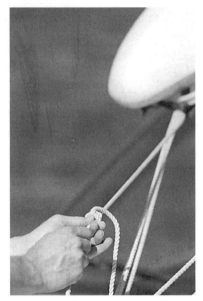

Figure 172. Tying safety lines

Figure 173. Kayak secured for travel

Two knots used in kayak transport are the trucker's hitch and the taut line hitch. To tie the **trucker's hitch**, twist the line two times, bring a loop through the loop at the end of the twist, and tighten. The trucker's hitch is often used when attaching the grabloops to the car frame with 1/2" nylon or dacron line.

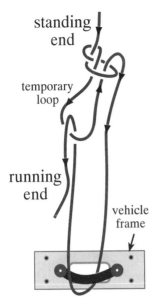

standing end

temporary loop

running end

vehicle frame

Figure 174. Trucker's hitch illustration

Figure 175. Trucker's hitch in use

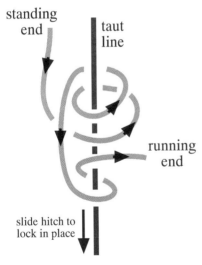

standing end

taut line

running end

slide hitch to lock in place

Figure 176. Taut line hitch illustration

The **taut line hitch** is performed by making two turns around the taut line with the running end, and completed by making an underhand loop around the taut line below the standing end's first point of contact with the taut line. We secure the taut line hitch by sliding the hitch along the taut line until the hitch holds tight. Because the taut line hitch is subject to slippage over long traveling distances, a safety knot, like a bowline, should be tied to a point on the car with the extra length of running end.

A **fisherman's knot** can be used to secure the line to the frame of the car. To tie a fisherman's knot, the paddler makes two loose loops with the running end through a metal ring. Then, the paddler wraps the running end around the standing end and brings the running end through the loose loops. To finish the fisherman's knot, the paddler turns an underhand loop around the standing end above the loose loops. Having two contact points with the car frame distributes the load along the metal ring. The excess running end should be tied off with additional underhand half-hitches around the standing end.

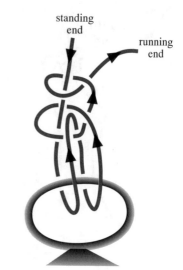

Figure 177. Fisherman's knot illustration

This combined hitch configuration works great for locking down a kayak because the trucker's hitch increases pulling force, the taut line hitch locks the line in place, and the fisherman's knot provides a solid anchor to the car's chassis.

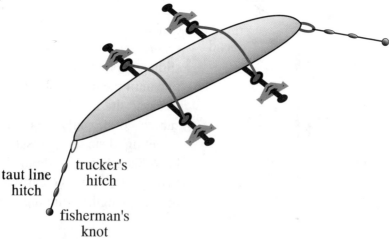

taut line hitch

trucker's hitch

fisherman's knot

Figure 178. Transporting kayak configuration overview

As River Paddlers, we must know how to read the river to avoid damaging the kayak and to ensure our safety. "**Reading the river**" is another way of saying, "determining the safest navigational passageway through potential hazards found on the river." This passageway, usually the highest body of flowing water, can generally be found in midstream in a straight channel, and toward the outer edge around a bend.

Figure 179. Scouting the river with a river map

Scouting a river before running it is invaluable for locating the best passageway. "**Scouting the river**" means to physically visit a section of river, paying particular attention to river obstructions, such as: rocks, logs, branches, shallow water, and unmanageable water.

Figure 180. Scouting the river for hidden obstructions

Having a **detailed river map** will prove useful in the scouting process. We recommend speaking with experienced paddlers about the visible and hidden obstructions in the river.

"The Kayak Express!"
River Scouting Report
Androscoggin River, Errol, NH

1. Calm water just below dam. Water moving slowly - can see water begin to move around bend.
2. Class 1-2 water. Rocks, white water. Nice trees on other side. Small paths to water from campground.
3. Scout from bridge. Class 3 below. Can see class 2 upstream. Can see class 3 upstream and downstream. Above and below water river obstructions are here.
4. Generally class 2-3 water below bridge. Class 2 & 3 eddies.
5. View from opposite side of river. Class 2 & 3 standing waves. Rough water ferrying location.
6. Slow moving water. Flat. Nice reflections of pines across river.
7. Class 1 to 2 water transition. Excellent location for ferrying drill. Transporting kayak practice location.
8. Fast moving class 2 & 3. Good location for sideslipping drills. Class 3 filled with below-water river obstructions.
9. Overlook. Lunch stop. Class 2 water below.
10. Stationary to class 1 water upstream of islands and Brown Co. Bridge.
11. Brown Co. Bridge. Overlooks above standing waves. River rider & capsizing drill. Safe open-end downstream 'V'.
12. View from bank below Brown Co. Bridge. Big, safe standing waves.

note: map for reference purposes only
(river conditions subject to change)

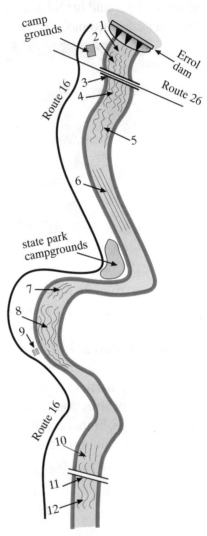

Figure 181. Androscoggin River scouting map

River obstructions can be identified by a paddler on the water through an understanding of the way water flows when in contact with above-water and submerged obstructions.

Flowing water tends to climb up objects that break the surface of the water - paddlers label this water formation a **cushion**. Experienced river team paddlers recognize an object just below the water's surface by the calm dark spot surrounded by flowing water - the calm spot over the rock is referred to as a **pillow**.

Figure 182. Cushion and pillow

A **hole**, or water which flows back on itself, indicates a very large rock is beneath the water's surface immediately upstream of this hole; beginner River Paddlers do well to stay clear of these because the hole tends to hold the kayak, often resulting in a capsize. More experienced River Paddlers, however, will often scout holes to be sure there is no trapped debris, then use the hole as a paddling playground.

Figure 183. Hole

A **horizon line** across a river is an indication of either a low head dam or waterfall formation. River Paddlers should portage around these river formations because of sharp dropoffs and the risk of striking unknown debris that may be trapped in or about these water formations.

Figure 184. Horizon line

Figure 185. Strainer

Strainers are large branches, above or below the water's surface, usually found in the river near the bank, especially to the outside of a river bend. Strainers hardly alter river flow and should be avoided at all cost. A River Paddler getting caught in a strainer will be forced under water by the river current; this can be fatal. If unable to avoid a strainer, the only chance for the river or swimmer paddler is to reach up and climb onto the strainer.

Figure 186. Eddy line and eddy

Lines separating rough water and calm water are **eddy lines**, where the smooth water sheltered behind the above-water river obstruction is referred to as an **eddy**. A pronounced eddy line is caused by the intersection of water flowing downstream in the main river channel and the water flowing upstream that constantly fills the void behind the river obstruction.

First-time River Paddlers are often surprised by the water current in the eddy that flows toward the river obstruction. The eddy current flowing upstream is only a fraction of the main river current, but often enough to require paddlers to gently control their kayaks while resting in the eddy.

Standing waves are caused by heavy water flow over objects, generally located a safe distance beneath the water's surface. Standing waves can hide other river obstructions, so paddlers should seek a high viewing point when scouting this type of water formation.

Figure 187. Standing waves

A 'V' with its open end downstream - **upstream pointing 'V'** - lets us know an object to be avoided is at the 'V's point, closest to us when approaching this water formation. The calm water behind the river obstruction causing the upstream pointing 'V' can be used by paddlers as a rest stop and scouting location.

Figure 188. 'V' - open end downstream

A '**V**' with its open end upstream - **downstream pointing 'V'** - is a sign that water is being forced between two objects. This rough, fast water flowing through the objects is called a chute. Paddlers should steer through a **chute** like this and enjoy the ride!

Figure 189. 'V' - open end upstream (chute)

The reason River Paddlers take the time to learn to recognize water formations associated with their respective river obstructions is to safely navigate the river. As we learned about river obstructions, paddlers on the river cannot always see river obstructions from the low vantage point of their kayaks - for example, a pillow may be hidden by standing waves immediately upstream. In response to this limited viewing angle, river paddlers have developed a set of **universal signals** over the years to enable a scouter on the shore downstream to tell those about to paddle a section of river where to pass to avoid river obstructions.

Figure 190. Universal signals - river right

Figure 191. Universal signals - river left

Figure 192. Universal signals - river middle

Four universal signals with which river paddlers should be familiar is "**river right!**", "**river left!**", "**river middle!**", and "**stop!**" The scouter uses the universal signals to indicate direction with respect to the river's direction of flow. So, if the paddlers can most easily and safely navigate the river to river left, the scouter will point to river left and the paddlers will steer their kayaks to port as they paddle forward with the river's current.

Figure 193. Universal signals - stop

A difficult situation is, of course, a **river capsizing**. If the paddler is unable to perform a successful roll, the paddler will wet exit. The **capsized paddler** should get his or her feet to the water's surface, face downstream, get to the upstream end of the kayak, roll the kayak cockpit face up, angle it 30° toward the closer river bank, and use the river's current to help in swimming the kayak to the river bank.

Figure 194. Capsized paddler - stay upstream of kayak

We should note that a swamped kayak can have the effective weight of more than several hundred pounds in moving water, which is why staying upstream of the kayak is highly encouraged. The capsized paddler should squeeze the kayak's grabloop as if it is a single piece of line, being careful not to place his or her fingers inside the loop because the river's turbulence can spin or roll the kayak, causing the loop to tighten around the hand or fingers. Above all else, remain calm and wait until reaching the river bank before attempting to stand.

Figure 195. River capsize - stay with kayak and hold paddle

The reason a capsized paddler should make an attempt to stay with, and upstream of, a kayak is that *a kayak is much less likely to be forced underwater than a lone swimmer*. Staying with the kayak will also make receiving help and reaching the river bank easier. Also, the capsized paddler should make an attempt to hold the paddle, as finding it later may prove to be difficult and time consuming.

Figure 196. Rescue paddler approaches capsized paddler

A **river rescue paddler** can approach the capsized paddler with the rescue kayak's bow or stern. Once the capsized paddler has control of the grabloop (squeezing as if a single piece of line), the rescue paddler will ferry to the nearest river bank. A rescue

Figure 197. Capsized paddler holds grabloop

paddler should talk to the capsized paddler and assure him or her that everything will be all right and to remind him or her not to stand until reaching the river bank.

Figure 198. Tow the capsized paddler to shore

Now let's discuss the safety responsibilities of a paddler who finds him or herself in the river without the kayak. First, do not panic. If you relax, you may actually enjoy the ride. Next, get into the **River Rider position**, which is on your back, with feet leading downstream and up at the water's surface. This position prepares us to fend off

Figure 199. River rider rescue using throw bag

obstructions and ensures that our legs stay clear of riverbed rocks; getting feet or legs trapped between or beneath riverbed rocks will hold the river rider beneath the water's surface and can be fatal.

If the **River Rider** must go it alone, he or she should stay in River Rider position, use the river's power by angling about 30° toward the

Figure 200. River rider position - feet downstream and up

river bank, and hand paddle to shore. A **river bank rescuer** should place his or her back foot on the throw bag line's end, hold the line with the non-throwing hand, toss the bag over the River Rider's head, lean

Figure 201. Throw bag toss - stand on line

down and back when pulling, and check the River Rider for signs of hypothermia and shock once safely ashore.

Experienced River Paddlers always paddle with others, check to be sure the equipment is properly prepared for the day on the river, and paddle in the company of an experienced scout. Rescue procedures and individuals' responsibilities are discussed prior to paddling. Finally, *River Paddlers never underestimate the power of moving water*.

Figure 202. Rescue position - down and back

Figure 203. Rescue complete - continue downstream

River Paddler Strokes

- put-in
- peel-outs
- shooting the rapids
- ferrying
- 'S' turns
- eddy turns
- surfing

In the River Paddler Strokes section, we will be learning the combination stroke skills used to control the kayak while running the river. We will find our flat water paddling practice during the Beginner, Intermediate, and Advanced sections to be valuable in navigating the white water. And, similar to flat water paddling, but even more important in white water paddling, is the concept of teamwork. At all times throughout the paddling day, one member of the paddling team or group who is experienced at river rescues must be in a position to assist another paddler in the event of a capsize, which is one form of **River Paddler teamwork**.

To begin river paddling, River Paddlers will **put-in**, or set the kayak into the river water, at a river bank at a calm water location, or, if the river current is strong, in an area of water protected from the downstream river current by a sufficiently large river obstruction. Recall from the River Paddler Practical section that an almost stationary pool of water distinguished from the main channel of flowing water is referred to as an eddy. We should also recall that the eddy water is actually flowing, mainly toward the river obstruction, so when entering the kayak, paddlers should set the kayak parallel to the river bank and use the paddle to maintain firm contact with the shore, just as we learned in the Beginner Strokes section. Once all the paddlers are in their kayaks, the group can choose lead and trailer paddlers. These two paddlers should have significant river paddling experience and, hopefully, paddling experience on the river the group is paddling.

Let's begin our river learning experience with a relatively simple drill known as ferrying. **Ferrying** is used to traverse back and forth across the river. Like any new skill, we first practice in a section of river that we can handle to build some confidence.

Figure 204. Ferrying - starting from an eddy

When leaving the eddy to begin ferrying, the kayak will be angled almost directly upstream. The paddler accelerates across the eddy line by using strong forward power strokes. The paddler may need to use a strong sweep on the direction-of-ferry side to prevent the kayak from being turned downstream. Strong power strokes and angle-correcting forward sweeps are the primary strokes used while ferrying. Paddlers should avoid using a paddle blade as a rudder to correct the kayak's angle since ruddering reduces forward momentum, enabling the river to push the kayak downstream.

While ferrying, the River Paddler angles the kayak's bow between 0° and 30° upstream toward the river bank he or she wishes to reach. River Paddlers should practice ferrying across the river in both directions, and facing downstream. River Paddlers should learn to use the moving water more than paddler power to traverse

Figure 205. Ferrying overview - lean downstream and angle

111

across the current before continuing downstream to more active sections of river.

One of the many skills (that will soon become second nature) a novice River Paddler learns while practicing the ferrying drill is the downstream lean. The **downstream lean** prevents the moving water rushing under the kayak from rolling the kayak to the upstream side, which can result in a capsizing situation.

Figure 206. Ferrying - maintain angle

Figure 207. Ferrying - use current

Once confident with the ferrying skill, paddlers should welcome the challenge of playing in rougher water. In faster flowing water, the downstream lean becomes essential to prevent the water rushing under the kayak from rolling the kayak to the upstream side. Leaning forward to lower the center of gravity makes the kayak more stable and adds weight to the bow, which assists in keeping the kayak pointed in the desired direction.

Another important skill with which River Paddlers should familiarize themselves is the eddy turn. An **eddy turn** provides paddlers with a means of getting their kayak behind a river current obstruction, such as a large above-water rock, to allow for rest and/or scouting of the next section of river.

Before learning the eddy turn, let's understand **river current dynamics**. The river current flows downstream and around, over, or even under obstructions, as we saw in the River Paddler Practical section. Immediately behind a river current obstruction the water must flow around, such as a large above-water rock, the

Figure 208. Low brace eddy turn overview

calm water (referred to as an eddy) actually flows upstream. At the intersection of the water flowing downstream and upstream, there is **hydraulic friction**, creating the water formation we refer to as the eddy line.

River paddlers use two basic stroke combinations when making eddy turns: one employs the low brace, and the other uses the Duffek stroke. In the first eddy turn stroke combination, the River Paddler will begin with a forward sweep and finish with a low brace. During the **low brace eddy turn combination**, the River Paddler uses the forward power stroke to paddle toward the eddy line at an angle of 45°, leans into the turn while making a strong forward sweep as the bow crosses the eddy line, and continues the lean into the turn. Once one-half of the kayak has crossed the eddy line, the turn-to blade is placed in the low brace position on the eddy water. The forward sweep and low brace in combination

Figure 209. Low brace eddy turn - paddle strongly across eddy

Figure 210. Low brace eddy turn - place blade in eddy

should be easy for us after our flat water paddling practice, but in the case of making an eddy turn, the stroke combination requires careful timing, which is dictated by several factors, including: the strength and velocity of the moving water, the velocity of the kayak relative to the moving water, the position of the river-current obstruction relative to its surroundings, and our own river paddling experience.

Starting the turn too early can result in the kayak's striking the eddy line with too little angle. The eddy current water flowing upstream and river current water flowing downstream will act together to continue turning the kayak back into the downstream moving water, usually resulting in a failed eddy turn and leaving the paddler floating backward downstream.

Figure 211. Low brace eddy turn - lean into turn

Figure 212. Low brace eddy turn - set position to stay in eddy

The River Paddler successfully crossing the eddy line uses the low brace, placed in the eddy's calm water, to keep the upstream-moving eddy current water flowing beneath the kayak from actually capsizing the kayak to the downstream side. In conjunction with the low brace, of course, the River Paddler should lean into the eddy turn as if riding a bicycle.

In the second eddy turn, the **Duffek stroke eddy turn combination**, the River Paddler will begin with a forward sweep and finish with the Duffek stroke. The timing remains the same; the River Paddler performs strong power strokes into the eddy between a 30° and 45° angle and does a forward sweep when the bow is crossing the eddy line. The Duffek stroke blade is placed into the eddy water once one-half of the River Paddler's kayak has crossed the eddy line. Like the low brace in the first eddy turn combination, the high brace of the Duffek stroke provides righting force if the River Paddler leans more than necessary to compensate for the upstream flowing eddy water current. The high brace also acts as a pole about which the kayak will spin. And, as in the low brace eddy turn combination, the River Paddler, during the Duffek stroke eddy turn, leans into the turn as if riding a bicycle.

Figure 213. Duffek stroke eddy turn

We should note that the stronger the river current, the stronger the eddy current. So, a strong eddy turn in a strong river current can get the kayak to turn and stop on a dime, which can be a rather exciting experience. In addition, shallow water is a compelling reason for a River Paddler to choose to use the low brace eddy turn combination over the Duffek stroke eddy turn combination; striking the river's bottom can be very disruptive to a Duffek stroke! Finally, before moving on to the other River Paddler paddling skills, we should practice and be very comfortable with eddy turns using both stroke combinations.

Low brace eddy turn

Figure 214. Low brace eddy turn - start turn with forward sweep

Figure 215. Low brace eddy turn - place low brace in eddy

Figure 216. Low brace eddy turn - lean into turn

Figure 217. Low brace eddy turn - rest and scout from eddy

Duffek stroke eddy turn

Figure 218. Duffek stroke eddy turn - start turn with forward sweep

Figure 219. Duffek stroke eddy turn - place blade in eddy

Figure 220. Duffek stroke eddy turn - lean into turn

Figure 221. Duffek stroke eddy turn - rest and scout from eddy

After using the eddy as a resting area or river scouting location, River paddlers perform what is known as a peel-out to re-enter the downstream moving water.

A **peel-out** is the reverse of an eddy turn in many ways. To perform a peel-out, paddlers give their kayaks some forward momentum to successfully free themselves of the eddy. The kayak is angled between 30° and 45° from upstream in the direction the paddlers wish to turn. When peeling out, River Paddlers lean downstream to prevent the water rushing under the kayak from capsizing them to the upstream side. As in the eddy turn, the River Paddler can use either stroke combination - either a forward sweep into a low brace, or a

Low brace peel-out   **Duffek stroke peel-out**

Figure 222. Peel-out - paddle strongly across the eddy line

Figure 223. Peel-out - strong sweep and lean downstream

Figure 224. Peel-out - maintain lean while performing low or high brace

forward sweep into a Duffek stroke. River Paddlers should plan a peel-out according to river strength, water depth, their paddling abilities, and impending paddling needs.

Figure 225. Peel-out - forward sweep and lean

Figure 226. Peel-out - place blade in downstream moving water

Figure 227. Peel-out - finish with forward stroke

Figure 228. Peel-out overview

119

Now that we are familiar with eddy turn and peel-out stroke combinations, we are ready to learn the 'S'-turn, used to cross from one river bank to the other. This second method is referred to as the **'S'-turn** because from overhead, the River Paddler's path will look like an 'S'. Unlike the ferrying exercise we started during our day on the river, River Paddlers paddle with the river for a short period when using the 'S'-turn. Although the 'S'-turn is often used to cross heavy rapids, as good novice River Paddlers, we should learn and practice on a gently flowing section of the river before advancing to rougher water.

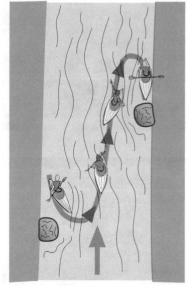

Figure 229. S-turn overview

Figure 230. 'S'-turn - start in near side eddy

Figure 231. 'S'-turn - peel-out

To begin the 'S'-turn, paddlers peel-out of the eddy, paddle at a 30° to 45° angle from downstream toward the opposite side river bank, and complete the 'S'-turn with an eddy turn in a pre-scouted eddy on the opposite side river bank. During the crossing, paddlers must lean downstream in accordance with the strength of the river current, make each forward power stroke count, and be prepared to use either a low or high brace to prevent an undesired capsize when performing an eddy turn in the far side eddy.

Figure 232. 'S'-turn - complete with eddy turn

Figure 233. 'S'-turn - lean downstream entire way

Figure 234. 'S'-turn -paddle across river current channel

Figure 235. 'S'-turn - meet at far side eddy

Experienced River Paddlers find surfing standing waves and holes to be great fun. **Surfing**, as referred to in river paddling, means keeping the craft stationary on the rushing water while using very little paddling power. To start, we need a section of the river with good sized standing waves, and maybe even a hole formation, which means that we will likely be paddling Class 3 white water.

From the safety of a nearby eddy, we paddle up and directly into the downstream flowing water. A single strong forward sweep may be necessary immediately after entering the fast flowing water to prevent the kayak from being turned downstream. Once the kayak's bow faces directly upstream in the flowing water, strong forward strokes and a proper lean are used to ferry across the water onto a large standing wave or to paddle directly forward into a hole.

Figure 236. Surfing - paddle from eddy into surfing zone

The trick to wave surfing is to get the bow beneath the rushing water to hold the kayak in place. Once being held in place, we should keep our elbows high to allow quick low brace reaction time and can use the kayak paddle blades as a rudder to keep the bow facing directly upstream. Note that only while we are surfing (i.e., firmly being held in place by the hole or standing wave water) can we use the paddle blade as a 'rudder'. At all other times, the rudder will cause the kayak to rotate downstream.

Once the kayak is no longer held, it is easily spun sideways to the current, so leaning downstream and being prepared to perform a low or high brace to

Figure 237. Surfing - use blade as rudder when bow held under water

prevent capsizing to the upstream side really become important. Practice and losing our sense of fear will enable us to play in the water with more confidence.

Figure 238. Surfing - be prepared for low brace

Figure 239. Surfing - ferry back to eddy

The hole slide is another of the fun skills experienced River Paddlers practice. To perform a **hole slide**, the paddler paddles diagonally on top of a small hole water formation, leans downstream, places a low brace to the downstream side of the kayak, and allows the hole to move the kayak as it may, until the kayak is flushed free. A good choice of hole to play in is one (free of debris) that will flush out the paddler in the event of an unexpected capsize. While upright and until being flushed free, the River

Figure 240. Hole slide - paddle into hole and lean downstream

Paddler will enjoy being spun around by the hole, but the paddler must maintain a downstream lean and be prepared to lean on the low brace. The low brace blade is always placed on the upward traveling recirculating water if the kayak is positioned in the hole. Wearing a helmet when performing the hole slide is critical, but it is really just as important for every white water exercise.

Figure 241. Hole slide - place low brace on recirculating water

The low brace paddle should always be placed in the white foam immediately downstream of the hole. The white foam indicates recirculating water flowing to the surface in this hydraulic formation (i.e., hole). The low brace blade's downward force will be supported by this upward flowing water. The hole slide is an advanced river paddling skill that will take a River Paddler much practice to perfect, again, while accompanied by an experienced river paddler.

Figure 242. Hole slide - maintain low brace until flushed free

We now have skills for controlling the craft during ferrying across the river and for making our way into and out of eddies. Let's now look at the last of the basic river skills we will learn: shooting the rapids. While shooting the rapids, we keep our eyes downstream, allow the kayak to rock and roll fluidly beneath us, and make each stroke count.

The challenge in shooting the rapids is recognizing and avoiding river obstacles. River Paddlers find the most successful preparation for shooting the rapids to be proper scouting of the river *before entering* the rapids, successful reading of the river *while in* the rapids, and using good eddy turn / peel-out / ferrying techniques *while navigating* the rapids. The strength of the river will determine the amount of scouting necessary. Speaking with people experienced with the flow of the river can provide information about obstacles and types of debris that can be found on the river and along the river banks.

Figure 243. Speak with local river enthusiasts

We should be aware of river flow changes ahead so as not to inadvertently paddle into a section of river beyond our paddling expertise. If paddling on an unfamiliar river, we should try to visually inspect the entire river run planned and take notes on our river map for later reference. If a complete visual inspection is not possible, we should be prepared to stop at any sign of river strength change, such as a narrowing of the river banks, a sharp bend in the river, a sudden increase of water speed, or a growing sound of white water.

Figure 244. Scout from different vantage points

Spotting a downstream 'V' to shoot can sometimes be tricky in faster flowing, more turbulent water, so paddlers will want to scout the river from different angles and heights, if possible. In addition to looking for a downstream 'V', we will also look for water formations that may challenge our paddling skills or allow us to practice a skill, such as a tight eddy turn. Much fun can be had while scouting and planning our safe river passage. Paddlers can challenge themselves by selecting passages that are flowing faster, have larger standing waves, or include several different water formations.

Figure 245. Scout upstream and downstream to locate hidden obstructions

The lead paddler will use his or her river scouting knowledge to guide the river expedition, keeping the other paddlers' skills and river paddling experience in mind when determining the paddling line to run. The lead paddler should make the decisions about when, and in which eddies, to stop, so as to enable additional scouting. The trailer paddler must be prepared to assist a capsized paddler, while the lead paddler locates an eddy for the non-assisting paddlers.

Figure 246. Designate leader and trailer paddlers before starting expedition

127

Figure 247. Shooting the rapids - paddle through the 'V'

Figure 248. Shooting the rapids - make each stroke count

Figure 249. Shooting the rapids - be prepared to use low and high braces

Figure 250. Shooting the rapids - keep kayak directed downstream

Figure 251. Shooting the rapids - focus downstream

Figure 252. Shooting the rapids - continuously stroke

Figure 253. Shooting the rapids - stay loose

Figure 254. Shooting the rapids - enjoy the ride

Once a safe, deep channel has been determined, the River Paddlers steer into the channel and keep their kayaks pointed downstream by using strong forward power strokes and forward sweep strokes, when necessary. River Paddlers should find that placing the blade into the standing waves' peaks over which the kayak travels aids in successfully navigating the white water.

Paddlers cannot always spot every obstacle, so the River Paddlers must be prepared with the ability to quickly maneuver the kayaks. Here is where our reverse paddling drills become valuable. In the river, the reverse power stroke acts as our brake and enables us to back-ferry to a safer navigation channel. The lead paddler of the river expedition will steer the group to 'river right' or 'river left' based on his or her assessment of the highest water in which to ride.

Figure 255. Shooting the rapids overview

Remember, the open end of the 'V' marks the points between which the kayak should pass. Everything we have learned about kayaking is employed to make our river journey safe, fun, and exciting!

Congratulations on your efforts...

**...and thank you for helping us through-
out our Kayak Express with you!**

River Paddler Review

1. **River gear**. List five to ten items River Paddlers would find important to wear or put inside the kayak while paddling on a river.

2. **Selecting the river**. Selecting a river right for a paddler depends on many factors; most notable is the paddler's skill and experience on a river. (a) During which season do rivers tend to run highest? (b) Novice River Paddlers should begin on which class river (always in the company of an experienced River Paddler).

3. **Transporting the kayak**. Name three knots or hitches used in kayak transport. Strap a kayak to the roof of a car and use the knots to be sure the kayak(s) will stay on the car's roof.

4. **River obstructions and water formations**. (a) List as many natural and man-made river obstructions as possible that a River Paddler may observe when scouting and reading the river. (b) Now list some associated river current formations caused by the river obstructions.

5. **River rider**. (a) Describe the River Rider position and (b) explain why River Paddlers use it whenever floating in a river?

6. **Tossing a throw bag**. We learned to stuff the line into the throw bag to help avoid tangling the line. When tossing the throw bag, what precautionary measures can the rescuer take to ensure both his and the River Rider's safety?

7. **Ferrying**. (a) River Paddlers always lean (upstream/downstream) while ferrying across the river. (indicate correct choice). (b) Why is leaning in this direction important?

8. **Eddy turns and peel-outs**. Eddy turns and peel-outs are stroke combinations paddlers use to enter and exit eddies, respectively. (a) What stroke combinations do River Paddlers use for making eddy turns and peel-outs? (b) Why do River Paddlers lean into the turn as if riding a bicycle? (c) Why is it suggested that the blade be placed into the calm eddy water only after one-half of the kayak has crossed the eddy line?

9. **Running the river**. In a river paddling excursion, the most experienced paddlers should be where in the group?

10. **Shooting the rapids**. While shooting the rapids, experienced River Paddlers steer toward standing waves because they are an indication that the large rocks at the river's bottom are a safe distance beneath the water's surface. River Paddlers also steer toward 'Vs' pointing (upstream/downstream) because it indicates a high, safe channel, as well. (choose the correct answer). Note that standing waves are often part of defining the shape of this 'Vs' formation.

Bonus.
Teach others the sport of kayaking to re-enforce the knowledge you have gained through "*The Kayak Express!*" lessons!

Index

A

artificial respiration   69

B

bag type heaving line   90
beam   37
beam entry   45
blades   16
body position during pad-
    dling   29
booties   12
bow   15
bow deck   15
bowline   68
bungee cord   95

C

capsized kayak   16
capsized paddler   106
car rack system   95
carrying a kayak   18
center of the kayak   31
checklist of questions   72
choosing the correct paddle
    size   17
chute   104
clothing   13
Coast Guard approval la-
    bel   11
cockpit   15
cockpit coaming   15
cockpit coaming seal ring 37
common sense   14

control-hand   26
control-hand/support-hand
    coordination   27
cushion   101

D

dams   94
deep water entry   44
detailed river map   100
distress signals   14
downstream lean   112
downstream pointing
    'V'   104
draining the kayak   24
dry exit   21
drysuit   91
Duffek stroke   60
Duffek stroke eddy turn
    combination   116

E

eddy   102
eddy lines   102
eddy turn   113
edges   16
entering the kayak   20
Eskimo rescue   42
Eskimo rescue drill proce-
    dure   42
Eskimo roll   80
exposing the shoulder   55

F

faces   16
feathering   16, 27
ferrying   110

Beginner Review Answers

1. **Safety**. (a) Whistle (audible signal), visible signal, sun protection, shoes with non-skid soles, wetsuit, drysuit, first aid kit, sunglasses, PFD, big sponge for bailing water. (see pages 10-14); (b) thunder and lightning storm, fog, extreme cold, high winds, extreme heat and humidity, and strong water current away from shore.

2. **Kayak nomenclature**. Intangible: bow, stern, port, starboard, cockpit. Tangible: hull, bow deck, stern deck, grabloops, cockpit coaming, foam walls, foot pedals, foot pedal rail, seat, flotation bags, knee pads. (see pages 15-16)

3. **Paddle nomenclature**. shaft, grip, neck/throat, blade, edge, tip, power face, reverse face. (see page 16)

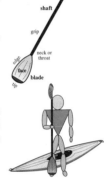

4. **Choosing a paddle**. One method of choosing the correct white water paddle size is to place a tip on your shoe; one arm's hand with the elbow bent 90° should be holding the center of the shaft when the arm is at the paddler's side. (see page 17)

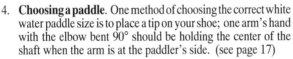

5. **Portaging the kayak**. Suitcase carry - keeps the other hand free to carry the paddle. Thigh carry - good for moving heavy kayaks short distances. Two-person carries - reduces carrying effort, and good for long distance carries. (see pages 18-19)

6. **Entering/exiting the kayak**. (a) Knees straight and toes pointed forward allows the paddler to enter/exit the kayak unencumbered. (b) By placing the paddle across the stern deck, setting the shore-side blade on land, and pressing down on the shaft, paddlers can keep a floating kayak stable and stationary on the water. (see pages 20-21)

7. **Wet exit**. (a) Tuck forward, hold the hull, lean over the water, exhale slowly out the nose, tap three times, give the thumbs-up signal, point toes, straighten knees, push hands against the stern deck, somersault forward, allow PFD to float you to surface. (b) The most important idea to remember is stay calm. (see pages 21-24)

8. **Forward power stroke**. Other causes of undesirable turning are unevenly positioned foot pedals, knees pressing unequally against the underside of the bow deck, uneven stroke lengths, blades passing at an angle through the water, and kayak lean (often caused by sitting toward one side). (see pages 27-30)

9. **Sweeps**. The sweeping blade should be as far away from the kayak as possible during the sweep strokes to provide mechanical advantage. (see rotating glass door analogy and pages 31-35)

10. **Straight line paddling**. Lean forward, keep the kayak from leaning by sitting in the center of the seat, be sure foot pedals are even, press against underside bow deck evenly with both knees (using proper knee protection), take long, even strokes, rotate shoulders, punch top hand directly toward the bow, be sure blades are perpendicular to kayak centerline when passing through the water, and look ahead at a stationary target. (see page 35)

Intermediate Review Answers

1. **Kayak physical dimensions**. Length, width, rocker, volume. (see page 37)

2. **Sprayskirt nomenclature**. (a) The sprayskirt fits snugly around the paddler's waist and the cockpit coaming. (see pages 37-38) (b) The sprayskirt's grabloop should always be available to the paddler in case a wet exit is necessary. (see page 39)

3. **Wet exit with sprayskirt**. Paddlers pull the spray-skirt forward then up to release the sprayskirt from around the cockpit coaming. (see pages 41-42)

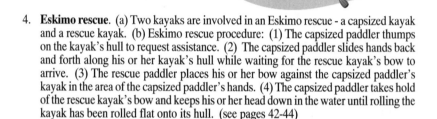

4. **Eskimo rescue**. (a) Two kayaks are involved in an Eskimo rescue - a capsized kayak and a rescue kayak. (b) Eskimo rescue procedure: (1) The capsized paddler thumps on the kayak's hull to request assistance. (2) The capsized paddler slides hands back and forth along his or her kayak's hull while waiting for the rescue kayak's bow to arrive. (3) The rescue paddler places his or her bow against the capsized paddler's kayak in the area of the capsized paddler's hands. (4) The capsized paddler takes hold of the rescue kayak's bow and keeps his or her head down in the water until rolling the kayak has been rolled flat onto its hull. (see pages 42-44)

5. **Kayak-over-kayak rescue**. The capsized paddler straddles the rescue paddler's stern in an effort to stabilize the rescue paddler's craft while the rescue paddler drains the capsized kayak (see pages 46-47)

6. **Moveable draw**. The sculling draw version of the moveable draw does not use a recovery because, as the blade slides toward bow then stern, its angle in the water constantly draws the kayak toward it. (see page 51)

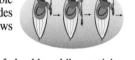

7. **Hip snaps**. A paddler's head should rest on his or her *left* shoulder while practicing hip snaps on port. (see pages 53-55)

8. **High brace**. During the high brace, the power face presses against the water. (see pages 55-57)

9. **Low brace**. A paddler's elbows are kept *high* when performing a low brace. (see page 58)

10. **Duffek stroke**. (a) The forward sweep on the port side should be used to start the Duffek stroke to starboard. (b) The paddler will lean on the high brace when using hips and legs to angle the kayak on its side during the Duffek stroke. (see pages 60-61)

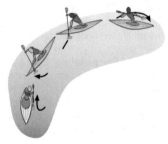

Advanced Review Answers

1. **Kayak materials**. A plastic kayak is more resistant to abrasions and cracks than a fiberglass kayak. A kayak is most often damaged by being paddled over or onto rocks or dragged on sand. (see page 65)

2. **Kayak characteristics**. (a) Shorter kayaks are generally easier to turn than longer kayaks. (b) Some kayak characteristics are acceleration, stability, surfing capability, rocker, storage, cockpit size, volume, and depth. (see page 65)

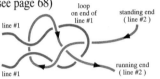

3. **Square knot**. Right over left, then left over right makes a square knot. (see page 67)

4. **Sheet bend**. The sheet bend should be used to tie two lines together. (see page 68)

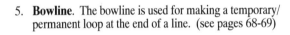

5. **Bowline**. The bowline is used for making a temporary/permanent loop at the end of a line. (see pages 68-69)

6. **Screw roll 1**. The screw roll can be broken down into four parts: rolling set-up, inverted position, uprighting set-up, uprighting combination. Of course, these parts are combined into one fluid motion. (see pages 71-72)

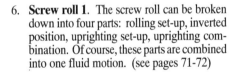

7. **Screw roll 2**. (a) The high brace is the stroke used during the screw roll uprighting combination. (b) The hip snap is also used during the screw roll uprighting combination. Recall that the hip snap is an integral part of the high brace. (see pages 75-77)

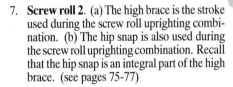

8. **Eskimo roll**. (a) The roll-side blade is extended away from the kayak during an Eskimo roll. (b) The farther from the kayak the blade is placed on the water during the rescue, the more mechanical advantage the paddler has over the kayak. (see page 80)

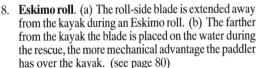

9. **Hand roll**. Keep hands cupped, perform strong, quick hip snap, bring head up last, arch toward the stern deck. (see pages 84-85)

10. **River simulation**. The kayak is moving forward during the river simulation self-capsizing method. The other self-capsizing techniques are performed while the kayak is stationary. (see pages 86-87)

River Paddler Review Answers

1. **River safety equipment.** A PFD, helmet, wetsuit or drysuit, spare paddle, throw bag, duct tape, first aid kit, drinking water, food, flotation bags, booties, neoprene gloves, audible distress signal, visual distress signal, river map, emergency phone numbers, or any other item or personalty that one might think useful or important. (see pages 89-92)

2. **Selecting the river.** (a) Rivers tend to run highest during springtime, when snow is melting into rivers and rain generally falls frequently. (b) Novice River Paddlers should begin on Class 1 rivers (always in the company of an experienced River Paddler). Once the paddling group becomes comfortable with paddling in constantly moving water, the group should progress to a Class 2 section and begin the ferrying, eddy turn, and peel-out drills. (see page 93)

3. **Transporting the kayak.** Three useful knots in kayak transport are the fisherman's knot, the trucker's hitch, and the taut line hitch. (see pages 95-98)

4. **River obstructions and water formations.** (a) Natural obstructions - rocks, logs, fallen branches, shallow water, cliffs; man-made obstructions - dams, bridges, kayak racing gates (poles suspended from wire over the river). (b) Rocks - pillow, cushion, eddy, hole, standing waves, V's; logs - cushion, pillow, hole; fallen branches - strainer; cliffs - waterfall, hole, horizon line; dams - horizon line, waterfall; bridges - V's, standing waves. (see pages 101-104)

5. **River rider.** (a) A River Paddler in River Rider position is floating on the back facing downstream with feet at the water's surface. (b) The River Rider position enables a River Rider to see above-water obstructions, to fend them off with the feet, and to avoid the trapping of a foot by a below-water river obstruction. (see pages 108-109)

6. **Tossing a throw bag.** When tossing a throw bag, place the back foot on the end of the throw bag line; keep weight low and back; do not wrap line around an arm or leg; toss throw bag beyond and at River Rider - throwing downstream may cause the River Rider to extend forward, which is undesirable in a river. The River Rider is better off back paddling to the throw bag. (see page 109)

7. **Ferrying.** (a) River paddlers always lean *downstream* when ferrying across the river (b) to prevent the water rushing under the kayak from capsizing the kayak to the upstream side. (see pages 110-112)

8. **Eddy turns and peel-outs.** (a) When performing an eddy turn or peel-out, the stroke combinations that can be used are a forward sweep and low brace, a forward sweep and stationary pivot, or a forward sweep and Duffek stroke. (b) River Paddlers lean into an eddy turn and peel-out as if riding a bicycle because the water being entered (i.e., eddy or downstream flowing river channel) can cause the kayak to capsize if the paddler is not leaning enough to counteract the rotation force the flowing water will exert on the kayak. (c) If the River Paddler places the blade that performs the low brace, stationary pivot, or Duffek stroke into the water before one-half of the kayak has entered the eddy, the kayak is likely to be spun by the eddy line currents, resulting in a failed eddy turn. A failed eddy turn results in the paddler's floating backward in the main river channel. Alert paddlers will use their ferrying skills to enter the eddy below where their turn would have put them had their eddy turn not gone awry. (see pages 112-119)

9. **Running the River.** The most experienced paddlers should be the lead and trailing paddlers. The lead paddler must be familiar with the river; the trailing paddler should be comfortable with performing a river rescue. (see page 127)

10. **Shooting the rapids.** River Paddlers steer toward and through 'Vs' pointing downstream because this type of water formation indicates that the water is flowing between obstructions to avoid. Note that a 'V' that points upstream indicates that a river obstruction is located at the farthest upstream point. (see pages 130-131)

International Scale of River Difficulty *

Moving Water Classifications

Class A: Water flowing under two miles per hour.
Class B: Water flowing two to four miles per hour.
Class C: Water flowing greater than four miles per hour.

White Water Classifications

Class 1:
Easy. Fast moving water with riffles and small waves. Few obstructions, all obvious and easily missed with little training. Risk to swimmers is slight; self-rescue is easy.

Class II: Novice
Straightforward rapids with wide, clear channels which are evident without scouting. Occasional maneuvering may be required, but rocks and medium sized waves are easily missed by trained paddlers. Swimmers are seldom injured and group assistance, while helpful, is seldom needed.

Class III: Intermediate
Rapids with moderate, irregular waves which may be difficult to avoid and which can swamp an open canoe. Complex maneuvers in fast current and good boat control in tight waves or strainers may be present, but are easily avoided. Strong eddies and powerful current effects can be found, particularly on large-volume rivers. Scouting is advisable for inexperienced parties. Injuries while swimming are rare; self rescue is usually easy but group assistance may be required to avoid long swims.

Class IV: Advanced
Intense, powerful but predictable rapids requiring precise boat handling in turbulent water. Depending on the character of the river, it may feature large, unavoidable waves and holes or constricted passages demanding fast maneuvers under pressure. A fast, reliable eddy turn may be needed to initiate maneuvers, scout rapids, or rest. Rapids may require "must" moves about dangerous hazards. Scouting is necessary the first time down. Risk of injury to swimmers is only moderate to high, and water conditions may make self-rescue difficult. Group assistance for rescue is often essential, but requires practiced skills. A strong eskimo roll (for kayakers) is highly recommended.

Class V: Expert
Extremely long, obstructed, or very violent rapids which expose a paddler to above average endangerment. Drops may contain large, unavoidable waves and holes or steep, congested chutes with complex, demanding routes. Rapids may continue for long distances between pools, demanding a high level of fitness. What eddies exist may be small, turbulent, or difficult to reach. At the high end of the scale, several of these factors may be combined. Scouting is mandatory, but often difficult. Swims are dangerous, and rescue is difficult, even for experts. A very reliable eskimo roll (for kayakers), proper equipment, extensive experience, and practiced rescue skills are essential for survival.

Class VI: Extreme
One grade more difficult than Class V. These runs often exemplify the extremes of difficulty, unpredictablilty, and danger. The consequences of errors are very severe and rescue may be impossible. For teams of experts only, at favorable water levels, after close personal inspection and taking all precautions. This does *not* represent drops thought to be unrunnable, but may include rapids which are only occasionally run.

* Used with permission of the White Water Affiliation, Phoenicia, NY.

Photographers

Robert Tannenbaum
Photographer

Len Harvey
Assistant Photographer

Amy Lynn
Contributing Photographer

"*Sailing's a Breeze!*" and "*Paddle to Perfection!*" are part of the Aquatics Unlimited "*Getting off the Ground!*" instructional watersport series. Both instructional boating courses are available in book, video, and water-safe quick reference guide formats. The videos are professionally produced, and the author-illustrated, photo-packed books provide students with questions and answers to measure learning progress. Great for beginners, intermediates, and those teaching others. SAB! and PTP! are book and video shelf musts! "*Waterskiing - Getting off the Ground!*" and "*The Kayak Express!*" are available in book format and offer the same quality and instruction.

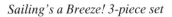

Sailing's a Breeze! 3-piece set

Paddle to Perfection! 3-piece set

Beginner

- ☐ safety
- ☐ safety equipment
- ☐ use of PFD
- ☐ nomenclature
- ☐ choosing a paddle
- ☐ portaging
- ☐ entering/exiting kayak
- ☐ wet exit
- ☐ draining the kayak
- ☐ using a paddle
- ☐ forward/reverse strokes
- ☐ turning theories
- ☐ forward/reverse sweeps
- ☐ paddling straight

Intermediate

- ☐ physical dimensions
- ☐ sprayskirt nomenclature
- ☐ using a sprayskirt
- ☐ spotter roll
- ☐ wet exit with sprayskirt
- ☐ Eskimo rescue
- ☐ deep water entry
- ☐ kayak-over-kayak rescue
- ☐ moveable draw
- ☐ sculling draw
- ☐ hip snaps
- ☐ high brace
- ☐ low brace
- ☐ stationary pivot
- ☐ Duffek stroke
- ☐ low brace turn

Advanced

- ☐ kayak materials
- ☐ kayak characteristics
- ☐ storing equipment
- ☐ square knot
- ☐ sheet bend
- ☐ bowline
- ☐ artificial respiration
- ☐ screw roll
- ☐ Eskimo roll
- ☐ board roll
- ☐ frisbee roll
- ☐ hand roll
- ☐ river simulation

River Paddler

- ☐ river gear
- ☐ selecting the river
- ☐ transporting the kayak
- ☐ transporting kayak knots
- ☐ reading the river
- ☐ scouting the river
- ☐ river obstructions
- ☐ universal signals
- ☐ river capsizing
- ☐ swimming the river
- ☐ ferrying
- ☐ eddy turns
- ☐ peel-outs
- ☐ 'S'-turns
- ☐ surfing waves and holes
- ☐ shooting the rapids